U0795389

READING INTO CHINA
漫读中华

文学经典
LITERARY CLASSICS

总主编◎刘　军
主　编◎耿小敏　滕永青
编　者◎蒋婷婷　王　斌　徐晓羽

外语教学与研究出版社
FOREIGN LANGUAGE TEACHING AND RESEARCH PRESS
北京 BEIJING

图书在版编目（CIP）数据

文学经典：英、汉 / 耿小敏，滕永青主编；蒋婷婷等编. -- 北京：外语教学与研究出版社，2019.12（2024.7 重印）
（漫读中华 / 刘军总主编）
ISBN 978-7-5213-1418-2

Ⅰ. ①文… Ⅱ. ①耿… ②滕… ③蒋… Ⅲ. ①汉语－对外汉语教学－语言读物 Ⅳ. ①H195.5

中国版本图书馆 CIP 数据核字（2020）第 005786 号

出 版 人 王 芳
项目策划 黄 骥
责任编辑 张思思
责任校对 闫智超
装帧设计 黄 浩
出版发行 外语教学与研究出版社
社 址 北京市西三环北路 19 号（100089）
网 址 https://www.fltrp.com
印 刷 北京协力旁普包装制品有限公司
开 本 787×1092 1/16
印 张 10.5
版 次 2020 年 2 月第 1 版 2024 年 7 月第 8 次印刷
书 号 ISBN 978-7-5213-1418-2
定 价 49.90 元

如有图书采购需求，图书内容或印刷装订等问题，侵权、盗版书籍等线索，请拨打以下电话或关注官方服务号：
客服电话：400 898 7008
官方服务号：微信搜索并关注公众号“外研社官方服务号”
外研社购书网址：https://fltrp.tmall.com

物料号：314180001

记载人类文明
沟通世界文化
www.fltrp.com

序

束定芳教授

中华优秀传统文化是中华民族代代相传的丰富遗产，是中华民族对人类文明的伟大贡献。随着国际文化交流的不断深入，逐渐加强中华优秀传统文化在语言教学中的融入，对促进跨文化交际具有重要的意义。在此背景下，“漫读中华”（*Reading into China*）系列丛书的推出应该是传承中华优秀传统文化、推进其国际传播的一次有益尝试。

Reading into China，可以理解为以阅读的方式走进中华民族文化；其中的*into*是一个动态介词，意在帮助读者全面地、深入探究式地、由古及今地认识和了解中华文化。丛书的中文名是“漫读中华”，以“漫”的方式阅读中华文明，品味中华文化的博大精深。

“漫读中华”系列丛书在内容上，从物态文化、制度文化、行为文化和心态文化等角度取材，体现了广义文化的内涵和外延。丛书在文本架构上以“中国故事”为着眼点，用文化链接的方式介绍了相关的中华优秀传统文化亮点，并与外国文化进行对比阅读，以此促进双向跨文化交际，帮助读者认识和了解中华民族文化，领悟中华文化和世界文化在形成和发展过程中的相互作用和各自特点，增强文化认同。

很多中华文化的表现形式是非文本的。“漫读中华”系列丛书在形式编排上注重图文并茂，使阅读内容更为直观和形象。所选图片包括典籍、画作、碑文等文化遗物，多选自博物馆展品或藏品，通过图释及相关阅读内容赋予这些陈列品鲜活的生命力，展现文物背后的文化内涵；也包括故居、古城、宫殿等文化遗迹，通过对相关故事或文化现象的阐述，增强读者对文化名胜的认知，让读者有身临其境的文化体验；还包括民俗、民间艺术、传统仪式等文化行为的图片，体现民族和区域特色的行为模式。

总之，“漫读中华”系列丛书有介绍、有对比，有梳理、有分析，有传承、有创新，是一套颇具特色的教材，也是一套深入浅出的文化普及读本。丛书的编写团队是一支勤勉钻研、善于思考，并对文化、语言和教学研究满含热情的中青年学者队伍。中华优秀传统文化的继承和传播需要这种钻研、思考和热情。

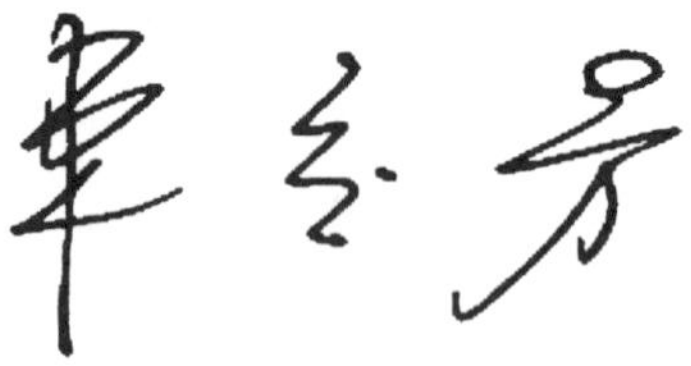

2018年8月3日

于上海

束定芳，上海外国语大学教授，博士生导师，上海外国语大学附属中学现任校长；外语类核心刊物《外国语》主编，海外语言学核心期刊*Journal of Pragmatics*等刊物编委；同时担任中国认知语言学研究会会长，全国高校外语学刊研究会秘书长。

前言

中华优秀传统文化是中华民族集体智慧的结晶，是人类文明的源头之一。讲好中国故事是新时代中国特色社会主义的命题和使命。“漫读中华”系列丛书以“源于中国，属于世界，基于历史，引领未来”为指导思想，使学习者在阅读故事的过程中理解中华优秀传统文化的内涵和表现形式，为用英语讲述中国故事、在国际交往中传承并弘扬中华优秀传统文化奠定基础。本系列丛书适合国内中、高级英语语言和文化学习者使用，亦适合对中国文化感兴趣的外国学习者使用；可用于课堂教学及学生课外自主学习。

本系列丛书包含历史故事、古代神话、民间传说和文学经典四个分册。丛书内容具有以下特点。

1. 选材广泛。丛书选材涵盖从远古到近代的哲学、科学、文学、医学、艺术等主题，选用能够展示中华民族智慧、勇敢、谦逊、礼让、大义等中华优秀传统文化的故事。

2. 结构合理。每个分册包含二十个单元。每个单元包括引言、故事、文化链接、讨论四个部分。故事内容短小精悍，采用图文结合的编写形式，符合现代阅读习惯。

3. 双语编写。采用英文和中文双语编写，方便课堂教学、自主学习和拓展阅读等。

4. 视角新颖。每个单元都编写了数条文化链接，通过扩充与故事相关的中华传统文化知识以及对比中外文化等内容，以点带面，提高学习者关于中华文化主题的语言应用能力和跨文化交际能力。

5. 思辨培养。每个单元均设计了思辨讨论，帮助学习者深入理解和分析中华优秀传统文化的内涵和特点，领悟中华文化在世界文化的形成和发展过程中发挥的重要作用。思辨讨论题亦可以作为演讲、辩论和写作等学习任务的主题。

“漫”本义指水向四面八方流淌，本丛书所有作者希望以中国故事为源头，链接中华文化，连贯中西文化本源，并希冀中华优秀传统文化在国际上的传播蓬勃发展，无远弗届。

Contents

目录

I THE MAN

Introduction

Classic of Poetry is the oldest poem collection in China; it is considered as the source of Chinese realistic literature. According to some scholars, it is Confucius who made the final editorial decisions for the poem collection. As one of the greatest works of ancient Chinese literature, *Classic of Poetry* has provided abundant inspiration for later poetic writing.

In *Classic of Poetry*, "The Man" is a narrative poem, and some of its traits can be seen in those poems written in the following thousands of years, such as "A Peacock Flying Southeast" and "The Everlasting Regret". The following story is adapted from this poem.

⊙ A Confucian temple with *Classic of Poetry* on the shelf, printed as an illustration in a Latin translation of Confucianism, Paris, 1687

Story Time

The man, goofily smiling, brought some cloth for thread, with a real intention of proposing marriage. Having sent him across the Qihe River, I lingered and said, "It's not that I would like to put it off, but that you didn't have a matchmaker by convention. I beg you not to be angry. We could fix the autumn as the day."

That autumn, climbing up the city wall, I waited for days. Finally, he was coming! We talked delightedly. He said, "I've attempted divination. Nothing unlucky at all! So, I came with the cart, in the hope of picking you up."

Before mulberry leaves turn yellow, how fresh they are! Turtledoves, do not eat the mulberries, which will intoxicate you. Girls, if you fall in love with men, they can do what they will, but a girl will never get away.

When mulberry leaves turn yellow, how sere they are! Since marrying him three years ago, I have shared his poverty all the time. The Qihe River would remember it once wetted the cart curtains as we crossed the river. I did nothing wrong, but he changed completely.

Never idle at home for three years, I wonder why he turned so rough. Not knowing what happened, my brothers joked with me as before. Alone, I could only lament my fate.

The Qihe River is very wide but has its shores. Since love has been the past, it would be better to let it end like this.

⊙ The Qihe River flowing through the present Qi County of Henan Province, mentioned 18 times in *Classic of Poetry*

Cultural Links

Classic of Poetry

Classic of Poetry includes over 300 poems dating from the beginning of the Western Zhou Dynasty to the middle of the Spring and Autumn Period. As one of the "Five Classics", which are representative works of Confucianism, it has been studied and recited by people for over 2,000 years.

Its content, mostly originating from oral chants, can be divided into three main sections: *feng*, *ya* and *song*. *Feng* is usually derived from ancient folk songs in various regions and reflects the voice of common people. *Ya* includes poems used by the aristocracy and government officials, and songs used at banquets. *Song* is often used in sacrificial rites.

Many Chinese idioms originate from *Classic of Poetry*, and some of them are used widely by people. Here are a few examples:

1) the fair maiden, the gentleman's good mate;

2) the full peach blossoms, bright and gorgeous;

3) her smile graceful, her eyes beautiful;

4) one day apart, as if three years passed;

5) hand in hand, with love to the end.

Fu, *bi* and *xing* in Chinese poetry

The three major literary techniques employed in *Classic of Poetry* are *fu* (straightforward narrative), *bi* (comparisons or metaphors) and *xing* (describing another thing before talking about the main content). *Fu*, *bi*, *xing*, *feng*, *ya* and *song* are together called Six Senses from *Classic of Poetry*.

In the poem "The Man", the first two verses describe the man's proposal and how the man and the woman got into marriage, which is *fu*. Then, the author compares beautiful girls to mulberry leaves, which is *bi*. The last verse first mentions the Qihe River has shores and then points out that love has come to an end, which is *xing*.

Homeric Hymns

Homeric Hymns is a collection of over 30 ancient Greek poems in heroic hexameters. The poems in *Homeric Hymns* range widely in length: Some include only three or four lines; some include more than 500 lines. Literary scholars seem to focus more on those long narratives, as well as some traits of oral literature.

The two most famous poems in *Homeric Hymns*, *Iliad* and *Odyssey*, are said to be created by Homer.

◎ *Apotheosis of Homer*, depicting the scene of Homer (two women beside him respectively symbolizing *Iliad* and *Odyssey*) being crowned by the Winged Victory, housed in the Louvre in Paris, France

Discussion

1. If you were a friend of the woman in the story, what would you say to her?
2. What are the similarities and differences between *Classic of Poetry* and *Homeric Hymns*?

壹　氓

引

《诗经》是中国最古老的诗歌总集，它被认为是中国现实主义文学的源头。根据一些学者所述，是孔子完成了该诗集最后的编撰和定稿。作为中国古代文学最伟大的作品之一，《诗经》给之后的诗歌写作提供了很多启发。

◎ 书架上放着《诗经》的孔庙，作为插图印制于1687年巴黎出版的儒家学说拉丁语译作中

《氓》是《诗经》中的一首叙事诗。从之后几千年的一些诗歌中，如《孔雀东南飞》和《长恨歌》，可见到此诗的一些特点。以下故事就是根据这首诗改编而来的。

故事

小伙子傻笑着带着布匹来换丝，真正的用意是求亲。我把他送过淇河，恋恋不舍地说道："不是我想耽误婚期，是你没有通常都会有的媒人啊！我恳请你不要发怒，我们可以把婚期定在秋天。"

那年秋天，我爬上城墙等了好几天。他终于来了！我们开心地聊着，他说："我已试着占卜过，一点凶兆都没有！因此，我就赶着车来，希望把你接走。"

桑叶未黄时，多么鲜嫩啊！斑鸠啊，别吃那些桑葚，它们会让你们醉倒。姑娘们，如果你们恋上男人，他们可以任意妄为，但女子将永远不能解脱。

桑叶变黄时，多么干枯啊！自从三年前嫁给他，我一直与其共苦。淇河会记得，在我们过河时，它曾溅了我们的车帷。我没做错什么，他却完全变了。

三年来，我在家里忙得团团转，我不知他为何变得如此粗暴。我的兄弟们不知道发生了什么，和以前一样开着我的玩笑。独自一人时，我只能哀叹自己的命运。

淇河很宽，但却有岸。既然爱情已经逝去，不如就让它这样终结吧。

◎ 流经现在河南省淇县的淇河
《诗经》中提及淇河十八次

文化链接

《诗经》

《诗经》包含西周初期至春秋中叶之间创作的三百多首诗作，作为儒家学说的代表作“五经”之一，两千多年以来一直被人们研究和诵读。

《诗经》的内容大多来源于口头吟唱，主要分成三部分：“风”“雅”和“颂”。“风”通常来源于古时候各地的民歌，反映老百姓的心声；“雅”包括贵族官吏所使用的诗歌和宴会乐歌；“颂”常用于祭祀典礼。

很多成语源自《诗经》，其中有一些被人们广泛使用，这里提供一些例子：

1）窈窕淑女，君子好逑；

2）桃之夭夭，灼灼其华；

3）巧笑倩兮，美目盼兮；

4）一日不见，如三秋兮；

5）执子之手，与子偕老。

中国诗歌中的赋、比、兴

《诗经》中所使用的三种主要文学表现手法是：赋（平铺直叙）、比（比较或比喻）、兴（在谈及主要内容之前先描述他物）。赋、比、兴、风、雅、颂并称《诗经》“六义”。

在《氓》这首诗中，前两小节描写男子求婚以及男子和女子如何结婚，这是“赋”。之后，作者将漂亮的姑娘比作桑叶，这是“比”。最后一小节先提到淇河有岸，然后指出爱已终结，这是“兴”。

《荷马史诗》

《荷马史诗》是三十多首古希腊诗歌的合集，这些诗歌都属于英雄双韵体。《荷马史诗》中的诗歌长度差别很大：有的仅有三四行，有的超过五百行。研究文学的学者似乎更关注那些长篇叙事诗，以及口头文学的一些特征。

《荷马史诗》中最著名的两首诗是《伊利亚特》和《奥德赛》，相传为荷马所作。

◎《荷马礼赞》
描绘了荷马（旁边两位女性分别象征着《伊利亚特》和《奥德赛》）被胜利女神加冕的场景
藏于法国巴黎卢浮宫

讨论

1. 如果你是故事中女子的朋友，你会对她说什么？

2.《诗经》和《荷马史诗》有什么相同之处和不同之处？

II THE DEBATE ON THE JOY OF FISH

Introduction

Zhuangzi, created by Zhuangzi (also called Zhuang Zhou) and his followers, plays a very important role in China's history of philosophy as well as literature, producing a far-reaching influence on later generations. It is renowned as the "philosophy in literature and literature in philosophy".

An anecdote between two great philosophers in the Warring States Period, Zhuangzi and Huizi, was recorded in *Zhuangzi*, from which the following story "The Debate on the Joy of Fish" is adapted.

⊙ *Zhuang Zhou Dreaming of Being a Butterfly*, painted on silk, 16th century

Story Time

One day, Zhuangzi and his friend, Huizi, took a walk along the bank of the Haohe River. Soon, they arrived at a bridge, where they had quite a good view of schools of fish swimming back and forth in the clear water.

"Look, the fish are swimming in the river happily and freely. How joyful they are! " said Zhuangzi, pointing to a school of fish.

"How do you know the fish are joyful since you are not one of them?" asked Huizi immediately.

"And you are not me. How do you know that I don't know the fish are happy?" retorted Zhuangzi, wittily throwing Huizi's question back at him.

But Huizi would not fall for it. He defended, "I am not you, so I don't know your mind. You are not fish, so you don't know the joy of fish, either. This is quite certain."

"OK, let's come back to the beginning. When you asked how I knew the fish were happy, you already knew that I did. To tell you the truth, it is right here, on the bridge above the Haohe River, that I knew the fish were happy. " After saying these words, Zhuangzi bent down and gazed at the water, totally being immersed in the joy of the fish.

◎ The Zhiyu Bridge, named after the debate on the joy of fish between Zhuangzi and Huizi, located in the Summer Place in Beijing

Cultural Links

The School of Tao and the School of Names

The School of Tao advocates living in harmony with Tao (which literally means "the way") and lays emphasis on inaction, naturalness and simplicity. Laozi and Zhuangzi are representative figures of the School of Tao.

The School of Names, also called the School of Forms and Names, emphasizes logic, laws, and the relation between names and forms. Huizi is one of the most influential figures of the School of Names.

The story "The Debate on the Joy of Fish" embodies totally different philosophical ideas of the two schools represented by Zhuangzi and Huizi. Zhuangzi focused on his inner connection with the outside world, which was realized through Tao, while Huizi tried to win the debate through clear logic.

Chinese idioms from *Zhuangzi*

The book *Zhuangzi* consists of a large number of anecdotes and fables, many of which illustrate the dialectical relationship between good and bad, largeness and smallness, life and death, and humans and nature.

Many Chinese idioms people use today are derived from the stories in *Zhuangzi*. "Blow hot and cold", "have a promising future", "be a mere copycat", "be a frog in the well", "go from bad to worse", and "be dumb as a wooden chicken" are all closely related to this classic work.

Zeno of Elea and Zhuangzi

Zeno of Elea, a philosopher in ancient Greece, put forth an interesting paradox.

Zeno's paradox is as follows: Supposing that one wants to get to the end of a path, he must first cover half of the total distance, then cover half of the rest, then cover half of ... and he can never reach the terminal in this way.

A similar paradox is mentioned in the book *Zhuangzi*: There is a one-foot stick and one takes away half of it every day; the stick could never be exhausted in this way.

⊙ Zeno's paradox

⊙ Zhuangzi's paradox

Discussion

1. What are the differences between the philosophical ideas of Zhuangzi and those of Huizi?
2. If you were a judge, how would you decide the result of this debate? Why?

贰　鱼乐之辩

引

《庄子》是庄子（也叫庄周）及其后学所作，在中国哲学史、文学史上都有极其重要的地位，对后世产生了深远的影响，被誉为“文学的哲学，哲学的文学”。

《庄子》中记载了战国时期两位伟大的哲学家庄子和惠子的一段轶事，以下“鱼乐之辩”的故事即改编于此。

◎《庄周梦蝶》
16世纪绢画

故事

有一天，庄子和他的朋友惠子沿着濠河岸边散步。没过多久，他们来到一座桥上，在这儿他们清楚地看到成群的鱼儿在清澈的河水里游来游去。

庄子指着一群鱼说：“瞧，这些鱼在河里游得悠闲自得，它们多么快乐啊！”

惠子立刻问道：“你又不是它们其中之一，你怎么知道鱼是快乐的呢？”

“你又不是我，你怎么知道我不知道鱼是快乐的呢？”庄子反驳道，机智地把惠子的问题抛回给他。

但惠子才不会上当。他辩解道：“我不是你，所以我不知道你的想法。你不是鱼，所以你也不知道鱼的快乐。这是很确定的。”

“好吧，让我们回到起点。当你问我如何知道鱼的快乐时，你就已经知道我知道鱼的快乐了。实话告诉你，我就是在这儿，在濠河的桥上，知道鱼的快乐的。”说完这些，庄子俯身观水，完全沉浸到鱼的快乐中去了。

◎ 知鱼桥
以庄子和惠子的鱼乐之辩而命名
位于北京颐和园

文化链接

道家和名家

道家倡导与“道”（字面意思是“路径”）和谐共处，强调无为、自然和朴素。老子和庄子是道家的代表人物。

名家，亦称“形名家”，重视逻辑、规律以及“名”与“形”的关系。惠子是名家最具影响力的人物之一。

“鱼乐之辩”的故事展现了以庄子和惠子为代表的两个学派完全不同的哲学思想。庄子关注的是通过“道”实现内心与外部世界的联结，而惠子试图用清晰的逻辑来赢得这场辩论。

《庄子》中的成语

《庄子》一书包含了大量的轶事和寓言，其中许多阐释了善恶、大小、生死、人与自然的辩证关系。

人们今天使用的很多成语就源于《庄子》中的故事。“朝三暮四”、“鹏程万里”、“东施效颦”、“井底之蛙”、“每况愈下”、“呆若木鸡”都与这部经典著作紧密相关。

芝诺（埃利亚）和庄子

芝诺（埃利亚）是古希腊的一位哲学家。他提出了一个有趣的悖论。

芝诺悖论是这样描述的：假设一个人想到达一条路的终点，他必须先走全程的一半，再走剩下路程的一半，再走一半……这样他永远也走不到终点。

《庄子》一书提到一个相似的悖论：一尺之棰，日取其半，万世不竭。

◎ 芝诺悖论

◎ 庄子悖论

讨论

1. 庄子和惠子的哲学思想有什么不同之处？

2. 如果你是裁判，你将如何判定这场辩论的结果？为什么？

III THE FISHERMAN

Introduction

Qu Yuan (also called Quzi) was a poet and statesman of the Chu State during the Warring States Period. Renowned as "the ancestor of Chinese poetry", he is the founding father of Chinese romantic literature.

The arrival of Qu Yuan's works announced the emergence of a new era in the history of Chinese poetry, and since then Chinese poetry has entered into a new stage of individual creation.

◎ *Quzi Humming Verses While Walking*, painted by Chen Hongshou of the late Ming Dynasty

Story Time

When Qu Yuan was in exile, he was wandering along the Yuanjiang River. He hummed verses as he walked, with a worn and haggard look. The Fisherman saw him and asked, "Aren't you the minister of the Chu State? How have you come to be in such a desperate state?"

"The whole world is muddy but I am clear. All people are drunk but I am sober. That is why I have been expelled," answered Qu Yuan.

The Fisherman said, "A sage will not keep a rigid attitude toward things; he will change with the times. Now that the whole world is turbid, why not stir up the mud in water? Now that all people are drunk, why not drink greedily with them? Why do you keep those deep thoughts and noble aspirations that are the very cause of your exile?"

Qu Yuan replied, "I hear that people who have just washed their hair must brush the dust off their hats before wearing them, and that people who have just washed their bodies must flick the dust off their clothes before putting them on. They would not have their bodies dirtied by unclean things. I would rather jump into the Xiangjiang River and bury myself in the bellies of fish than have my body polluted by the dirt of the vulgar world."

Hearing this, The Fisherman smiled and rowed away, singing, "The Canglang water is clear; it can be used to rinse my hat tassels. The Canglang water is turbid; it can be used to wash my feet."

The Fisherman went far away without saying anything more.

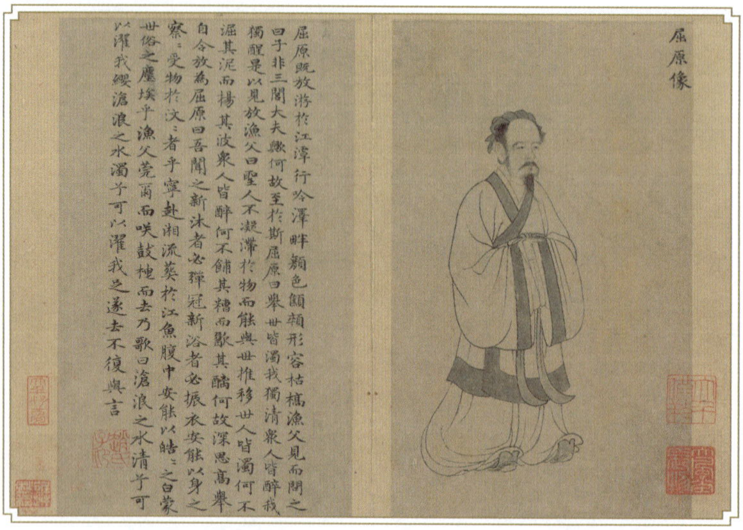

◎ "The Fisherman" from a Yuan Dynasty painting album after Zhao Mengfu, housed in the Metropolitan Museum of Art in New York, the United States

Cultural Links

The *chuci* style

The *chuci* style is a new poetic style created by some poets of the Chu State and its literary technique is based on romanticism. It left a trace in various realms of Chinese literature.

Liu Xiang of the Han Dynasty compiled major poems in the *chuci* style for a book titled *Verses of Chu*. It is a very important anthology of romantic poetry in the history of Chinese literature, and most of its works were created by Qu Yuan.

The fisherman, woodcutter, farmer and scholar

The fisherman, woodcutter and farmer are important professions in China's traditional agricultural society. Many scholars chose to retreat from the secular world, leading a life of a fisherman, a woodcutter, or a farmer.

For the Chinese, the fisherman, woodcutter, farmer and scholar are symbols of a reclusive life that pursues harmony and tranquility.

The Fisherman in the story gained an insight into world affairs, and chose to, in the

The Woodcutter Asking the Fisherman, painted on the Long Corridor of the Summer Palace in Beijing

disguise of a fisherman, be worldly-wise and play safe in the world of turbulence.

Four Great Cultural Celebrities in the World

In 1953, the World Peace Council held a conference in Helsinki, Finland, and called on people across the globe to commemorate the Four Great Cultural Celebrities in the World. They are the Chinese poet Qu Yuan, the Polish astronomer Copernicus, the French writer Rabelais and the British playwright Shakespeare.

Discussion

1. What are the differences between the life attitude of Qu Yuan and that of The Fisherman?
2. What are the major romantic literary works in the history of Chinese literature? What similarities do these works share?

叁　渔父

引

屈原（也叫屈子），战国时期楚国诗人及政治家，被誉为“中华诗祖”，中国浪漫主义文学奠基人。

屈原作品的问世，宣告了中国诗歌史上一个新时代的来临。自此，中国诗歌进入了个人独创的新阶段。

◎《屈子行吟图》
明末陈洪绶绘

故事

在遭到放逐时，屈原沿着沅江游荡。他边走边吟唱诗句，面容疲惫憔悴。渔父看见了他，问道：“您不是楚国大夫吗？怎么落到如此绝望的境地？”

屈原答道：“天下皆浊，独我清明；世人皆醉，独我清醒。那正是我被放逐的原因啊！”

渔父说：“圣人不会死板地对待事物，能随世道一起变化。既然整个世界都浑浊不清，何不搅动水中的泥浆呢？既然所有人都醉了，何不跟着他们畅饮呢？您为什么要怀揣着那些深刻的思想和崇高的志向？那正是您被放逐的原因啊！”

屈原回复道：“我听说刚洗过头的人在戴上帽子之前一定要弹去帽子上的尘土，刚洗过澡的人在穿上衣服之前一定要抖掉衣服上的泥灰。他们不会让自己的身体被污浊之物沾染。我宁可投身湘江，葬身鱼腹，也不愿令我的身躯蒙上俗世之尘埃。”

听了这话，渔父微微一笑，划船离去，唱道：“沧浪水清啊，可用来洗我的帽缨；沧浪水浊啊，可用来洗我的双足。”

渔父远去，不再说任何话。

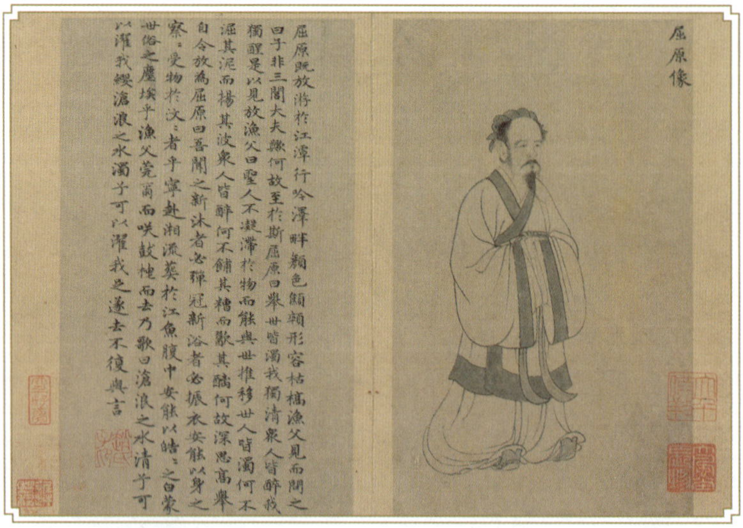

◎ 元代仿赵孟頫图册中的《渔父》篇
藏于美国纽约大都会艺术博物馆

文化链接

楚辞体

楚辞体是一些楚国诗人创作的新诗体，文学表现手法以浪漫主义为基础。它在中国文学的多个领域里都留下了印迹。

汉代刘向将重要的楚辞体诗歌辑录成书，书名题作《楚辞》。《楚辞》是中国文学史上一部非常重要的浪漫主义诗歌总集，全书大部分作品是由屈原创作的。

渔樵耕读

渔夫、樵夫、农夫是中国传统农业社会的重要职业。很多读书人选择远离俗世，过着渔夫、樵夫或农夫一般的生活。

对中国人来说，渔樵耕读是隐士生活的象征，这种生活追求和谐与宁静。

故事中的渔父洞察世事，在乱世中选择伪装成渔夫明哲保身。

世界四大文化名人

1953年，世界和平理事会在芬兰的赫尔辛基开会，号召全世界人们纪念世界四大文化名人。他们是中国诗人屈原、波兰天文学家哥白尼、法国作家拉伯雷以及英国戏剧家莎士比亚。

《渔樵问对》
北京颐和园长廊画作

讨论

1. 屈原和渔父的人生态度有什么不同之处?
2. 中国文学史上有哪些主要的浪漫主义文学作品？这些作品有什么共同之处?

IV CARVING ON THE MOVING BOAT TO FIND THE SWORD

Introduction

"Carving on the Moving Boat to Find the Sword" is a fable from "Studying the Present" in *Master Lü's Spring and Autumn Annals*. In "Studying the Present", the fable is taken as an example to prove the idea that "with fixed rules, a country will fall into absurdity". When the time and situation have changed, rules should be changed, too. If this principle is understood by everyone, mistakes can be avoided.

The following story is adapted from this fable.

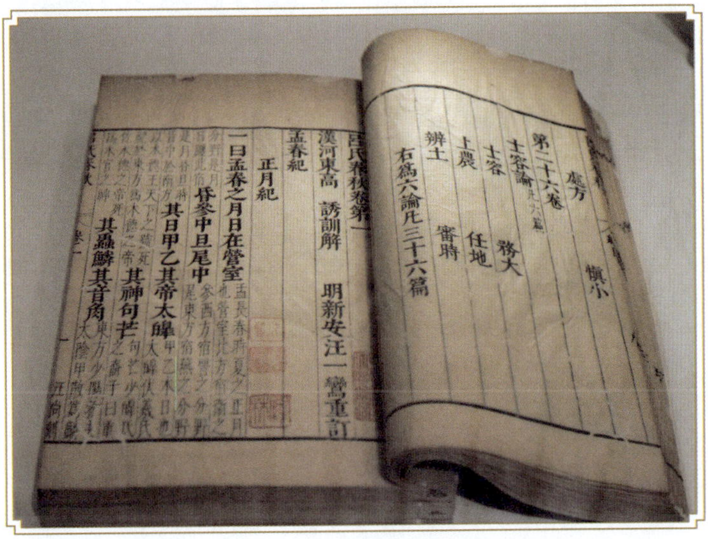

◎ *Master Lü's Spring and Autumn Annals*, housed in the National Museum of China

Story Time

One day, a man of the Chu State crossed a river by boat. Through his carelessness, his sword dropped from the boat into the water. Not in a hurry at all, he took out a small knife and made a mark on the side of the boat from which the sword dropped.

The boatman beside him asked, "Why don't you jump into the water at once to get your sword?" He pointed to the mark and said slowly, "There is no need to worry. The mark will help me to find the sword when we arrive at the dock." His confident words left the boatman wondering what would happen next.

When the boat reached the shore and stopped, the man dived into the river from the marked place on the boat to look for his sword. The boat moved but the sword did not move in the water. What a stupid way to look for the sword!

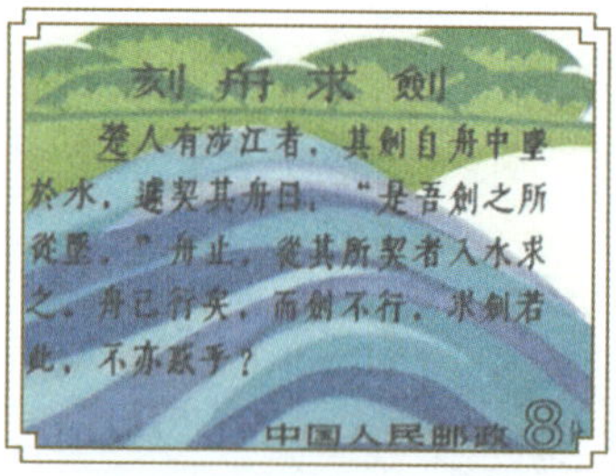

⊙ A set of stamps related to the fable "Carving on the Moving Boat to Find the Sword", issued by People's Postal Service of China (now China Post) on March 10th, 1981

Cultural Links

Master Lü's Spring and Autumn Annals

Master Lü's Spring and Autumn Annals is a classic compiled under the supervision of the Qin State Chancellor Lü Buwei. It was completed around 239 BC.

According to *Records of the Historian*, Lü Buwei exhibited the completed text on the city gate of Xianyang, and he also put up a notice that said any traveling scholar who could add or omit even a single word could be offered 1,000 taels of gold.

This classic collects ideas from the Hundred Schools of Thought (Legalism, Confucianism, Mohism, Taoism, etc).

The Chinese idiom "throw a baby into the river"

This Chinese idiom from "Studying the Present" in *Master Lü's Spring and Autumn Annals* supported the same idea.

One day, a passer-by saw a man trying to throw a crying baby into the river. He asked why the man did so. The man said, "The baby's father is a good swimmer, so the baby will certainly have no trouble in the water."

The use in *Dream of the Red Chamber*

At the end of *Dream of the Red Chamber*, when Cao Xueqin was asked why he was willing to relate the story, he responded as follows:

"It would be my pleasure to ... with a few friends ... There is no need to make formal comments or publish it. To make a thorough investigation as you did is like being the man of the Chu State who carved on the moving boat to find the sword or the man of the Qi State who played the zither with the peg glued." (Extracted from Chapter 120 of *Dream of the Red Chamber*)

The Indian fable "Losing the Bowl While Taking the Boat"

This is a similar fable in *One Hundred Buddhist Parables.*

Once upon a time, a man crossed a river by boat. His silver bowl dropped into the water. Immediately, he made a mark on the side of the boat. Two months later, the boat arrived at the Lion State and stopped. The man dived into the river to look for his bowl.

Discussion

1. Why couldn't the man of the Chu State find the sword in the river?
2. Is there any other example that can prove we should act accordingly? Please describe it.

肆　刻舟求剑

引

“刻舟求剑”是《吕氏春秋·察今》中的一则寓言。《察今》以这则寓言为例，证明了“守法而弗变则悖”的观点。

当时过境迁，规则也要改变。如果大家都理解这个道理，就能避免错误。

以下故事就是根据这则寓言改编而来的。

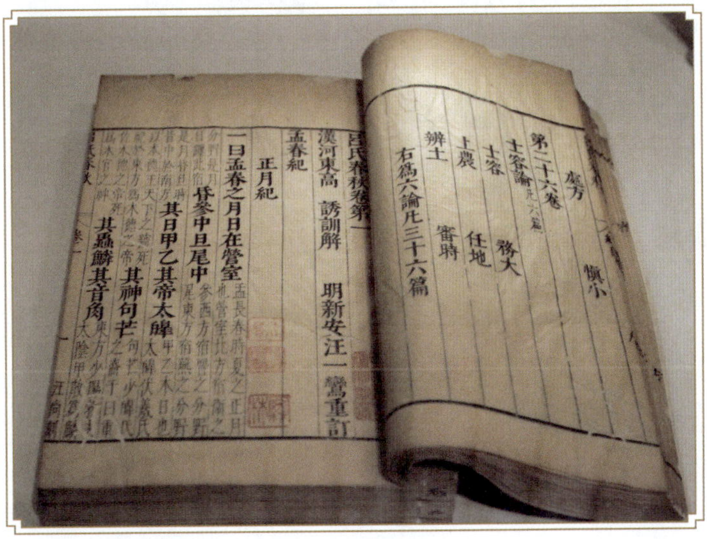

◎《吕氏春秋》
中国国家博物馆藏品

故事

有一天，有个楚国人乘船过江。由于他的疏忽，他的宝剑从船上掉到水里了。他一点儿也不着急，拿出一把小刀，在船舷上剑掉落的地方做了个记号。

他身旁的船夫问道：“你为什么不赶快下水把你的宝剑捞起来？”他指着那个记号，慢悠悠地说道：“不用担心，等船到了码头，这个记号会帮我找到宝剑。”他那充满自信的话语让船夫很疑惑接下来会发生什么。

当船靠岸停下，这个人从船上标记的地方跳进江里去寻找他的宝剑。船移动了，但是剑在水中并未移动。多么愚蠢的寻剑方式！

◎ 一套关于“刻舟求剑”寓言的邮票
1981年3月10日由中国人民邮政（现“中国邮政”）发行

文化链接

《吕氏春秋》

《吕氏春秋》是秦朝丞相吕不韦主持编撰的一部经典著作，大约于公元前239年完成。

据《史记》记载，吕不韦在咸阳城门上展示了编好的文本，还贴出了一则告示，声明任何门客只要能增减哪怕一个字，都可以获得千两黄金。

这部著作集合了诸子百家（法家、儒家、墨家、道家等）的思想。

成语“引婴投江”

《吕氏春秋·察今》中的这则成语佐证了同一观点。

有一天，一个路人看见有个人试图把哭着的婴儿扔到江里，就问他为什么这么做。他说：“这孩子的父亲擅长游泳，所以孩子在江里当然没问题。”

《红楼梦》中的应用

在《红楼梦》结尾处，当曹雪芹被问到为何他愿意传述这个故事时，他回答如下：

“乐得与二三同志……又不必大人先生品题传世。似你这样寻根究底，便是刻舟求剑、胶柱鼓瑟了。”（摘自《红楼梦》第一百二十回）

印度寓言“乘船失钵”

这是《百喻经》中一则类似的寓言。

从前，有个人乘船过河，他的银钵掉进了水里。他立刻在船舷上做了个记号。两个月后，船到达了狮子国，停了下来。这个人跳进河里去寻找自己的钵。

讨论

1. 为什么那个楚国人在江中找不到宝剑？
2. 有没有其他例子可以用来说明我们应该随机应变？请讲述一下。

V THE SPEAR-SHIELD PARADOX

Introduction

Spears and shields are weapons commonly used in ancient warfare, and they have completely opposite functions of attack and defense.

The Chinese idiom "the spear-shield paradox" can find its origin in the book *Hanfeizi*, and it is often used to criticize those who are inconsistent in their words or actions. The following story is adapted from this idiom.

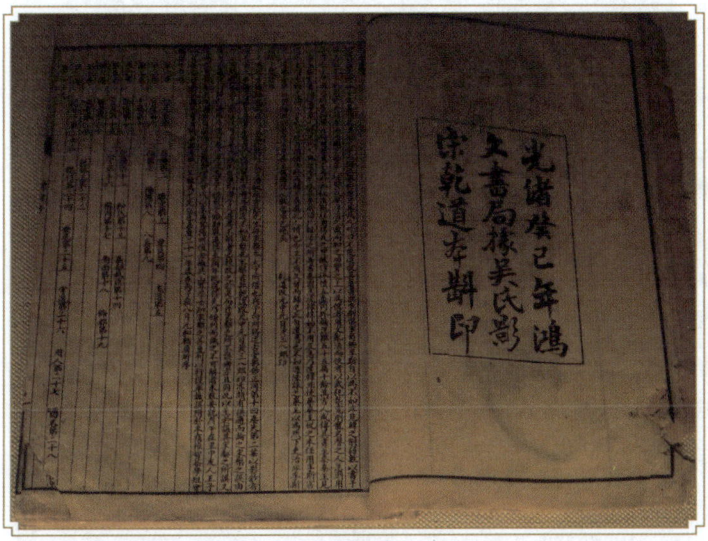

◎ An edition of *Hanfeizi* from the Guangxu Period of the Qing Dynasty, exhibited at the Hunan Museum in Changsha City of Hunan Province

Story Time

In the Chu State, a vendor was selling spears and shields at the market. As people approached, he began to tout loudly in order to sell more spears and shields.

"Come on! Look!" the vender held a spear aloft and said. "This is the sharpest spear in the world. It can pierce all shields."

More and more people were attracted by the loud voice. Seeing this, the verdor held a shield and delightedly continued, "Here! Look at this! This is the hardest shield in the world. It can defend against all spear attacks."

After this, a buzz of conversation was sparked among the crowd. All of a sudden, a man came up to the vendor and said, "Since you have the sharpest spear and the hardest shield, I wonder what would happen if you used your spear to pierce your shield?"

The vendor was struck dumb, unable to answer the question. Then, he quickly packed his spears and shields and left in embarrassment, and the crowd burst into laughter.

A stone statue of a man holding a spear and a shield, situated in Wuhan City of Hubei Province

Cultural Links

Zhuzi's prose

Zhuzi's prose refers to the prose written by scholars from the Hundred Schools of Thought, and it is characterized by careful reasoning, clear structure, plain words, etc.

Zhuzi's prose includes some well-known works such as *Analects, Mozi, Xunzi, Hanfeizi*, and *Master Lü's Spring and Autumn Annals*.

Han Fei and *Hanfeizi*

Han Fei is a well-known prose writer, thinker and philosopher of the late Warring States Period, and he is also a main representative of Legalism.

The book *Hanfeizi* mainly embodies Hanfei's philosophy of country administration. It consists of 55 articles and touches on administration, diplomacy, war, etc. According to the book, a ruler must follow three principles to maintain his reign: *fa* (law), *shu* (appropriate administrative techniques), and *shi* (possession of authority). The law must highly reward those who obey it and severely punish those who violate it.

Han Fei's philosophy had a profound influence on Emperor Qin Shihuang (the first emperor of the Qin Dynasty), who adopted Legalism thoughts and succeeded in unifying the whole country.

Chinese idioms from *Hanfeizi*

Apart from "the spear-shield paradox", there are many other Chinese idioms that originate from the book *Hanfeizi*. Here are two examples.

The idiom "keep the case and return the pearl" is often used to satirize those who attend to trifles and neglect essentials and thus make wrong decisions.

The idiom "play the *yu* (a musical instrument in ancient China) to make up the number" can be used to criticize those who are ignorant and incompetent but pretend to have great learning.

The Laelaps dog and the Teumessian fox

According to Greek mythology, Laelaps was a dog that could catch everything it hunted, and Teumessian was a fox that could never be caught. One day, Laelaps was dispatched to catch Teumessian. The chase lasted for a long time and finally Zeus realized their contradictory fates. Thus he turned them into stone and cast them into the stars.

Discussion

1. If you were the vendor in the story, how would you sell spears and shields?
2. Have you ever encountered or heard of a paradoxical situation? Please describe it.

伍　自相矛盾

引

矛与盾是古代战争中常用的兵器。矛用于进攻，盾用于防御，其作用完全相反。

成语“自相矛盾”源自《韩非子》一书，通常用来批评那些言语或行为前后不一的人。以下故事就是根据这个成语改编而来的。

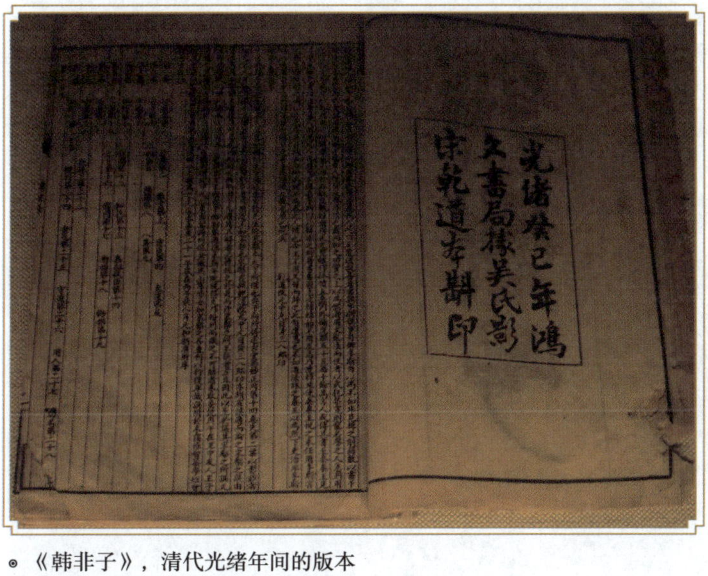

◎《韩非子》，清代光绪年间的版本
展于湖南省长沙市的湖南省博物馆

故事

在楚国，有一个小贩在集市售卖长矛与盾牌。有人过来时，他开始大声吆喝，以便卖出更多的矛和盾。

“来啊！看！”小贩高高举起一支长矛，说道。“这是世上最锋利的长矛，它可以刺破任何盾牌。”

高声吆喝吸引了越来越多的人。见此情景，小贩举起一块盾牌，开心地接着说道：“来！看这个！这是世上最坚硬的盾牌，它可以抵挡住任何长矛的攻击。”

此言一出，围观者议论纷纷。突然，一名男子走到小贩跟前，说道：“既然你有世上最锋利的长矛与世上最坚硬的盾牌，那么如果你用你的长矛刺你的盾牌，结果会怎样？”

小贩哑口无言，无法回答这个问题。然后，他迅速收拾好他的长矛与盾牌，灰溜溜地离开了。围观者哄堂大笑。

◎ 男子手持矛与盾的石雕
位于湖北省武汉市

文化链接

诸子散文

诸子散文指的是诸子百家的学者们所写的散文，有推理缜密、结构清晰、语言朴实等特点。

诸子散文中有一些著名的作品，比如《论语》、《墨子》、《荀子》、《韩非子》、《吕氏春秋》等。

韩非与《韩非子》

韩非是战国末期著名的散文家、思想家、哲学家，也是法家的主要代表人物。

《韩非子》一书主要展现了韩非的治国思想，包括五十五篇文章，涉及管理、外交、战争等内容。据该书所述，君主需遵循法（法律）、术（适宜的管理技巧）、势（对权力的掌控）三原则以维持其统治。法律必须厚赏守法者，严惩违法者。

韩非的理念对秦始皇（秦朝第一位皇帝）产生了深刻的影响。他接纳了法家的思想，成功统一了整个国家。

《韩非子》中的成语

除了“自相矛盾”以外，还有许多其他成语也源自《韩非子》一书。以下是两个例子。

“买椟还珠”这个成语通常用来讽刺那些因舍本逐末而作出错误决策的人。

“滥竽（中国古代的一种乐器）充数”这个成语可以用来批评那些不学无术却要装作学识渊博的人。

莱拉普斯犬和透墨索斯狐

据希腊神话所述，莱拉普斯是一只能捕获它所追逐的任何东西的犬，而透墨索斯是一只永远不会被捕获的狐。有一天，莱拉普斯被派去追捕透墨索斯。这场追逐持续了很久。最终，宙斯意识到了两者截然相反的宿命。于是，他将它们变成了石头，丢入群星之中。

讨论

1. 如果你是故事中的那个小贩，你会如何卖矛与盾？

2. 你是否经历过或听说过自相矛盾的情景？请讲述一下。

VI A PEACOCK FLYING SOUTHEAST

Introduction

"A Peacock Flying Southeast" is a long narrative poem. Its title comes from the first line of the poem, which is used to introduce the rest of the story. The image of "a peacock flying southeast and looking back every few miles" symbolizes the strong attachment of a young couple (Jiao Zhongqing and Liu Lanzhi) and their reluctance to part from each other.

This poem marks the maturity of ancient Chinese narrative poetry. The following story is adapted from the poem collected in *New Songs from the Jade Terrace*.

⊙ A picture of the rock-and-reed pledge, carved on a block of wood at the Cultural Park of a Peacock Flying Southeast in Huaining County of Anhui Province

Story Time

A peacock flew southeast, looking back every few miles.

One night, when Jiao Zhongqing, working far away, came back and had a short stay with his wife, the young wife wept, saying, "From 13 to 16, I learned to weave, to sew, to play the *konghou* and to read classics. At 17, I became your wife. Every day, I toiled at the loom till midnight, yet couldn't satisfy your mother. Please tell your mother to let me go."

Hearing this, Zhongqing's mother became furious and told her son that Lanzhi was not good enough for him. Zhongqing could do nothing but plead with Lanzhi to return to her maiden family temporarily.

At dawn, after decking herself out, Lanzhi bid farewell to her mother-in-law and sister-in-law and got into the carriage. Before she left, Zhongqing whispered, "Wait for me. I'll bring you back soon."

"May your love be as strong as the rock and mine as tough as the reed," replied Lanzhi.

Hearing that the pretty and virtuous young lady was divorced, matchmakers came one after another. Finally, Lanzhi yielded to her brother's pressure and agreed to marry a government official's son.

The wedding ceremony was very splendid. Zhongqing came hurriedly, and was broken-hearted. He said, "Congratulations! The rock is still strong, but the reed has lost its toughness. May you be happy. And for me, death shall be my destiny."

"Please be fair, Zhongqing. Both of us have been forced to accept our fate. Let's reunite in the other world," replied Lanzhi.

At dusk, Lanzhi plunged into a pond, while Zhongqing hanged himself from a tree in the southeast. In great grief and regret, the two families buried them together. Pines, cypresses and Chinese parasol trees grew thickly there, and amid the trees, two little birds sang to each other day and night.

◉ The Peacock Stand in Huaining County of Anhui Province, originally constructed in the Tang Dynasty, said to be where the love story of Jiao and Liu took place

Cultural Links

Yuefu

Yuefu originally referred to the music bureau set up by the ancient court, and it was in charge of the music used by the court and was responsible for collecting folk songs created by average people. Later, *yuefu* became a genre of poetry.

A *yuefu* poem usually has five-character lines. "The Ballad of Mulan" and "A Peacock Flying Southeast", known as "the twin pearls of *yuefu*", are considered by many to be the two best *yuefu* poems.

The Hostess of the Lujiang Family

In 748 AD, Li Bai, a famous poet in the Tang Dynasty, passed by an official's family in Lujiang County, where Jiao Zhongqing, the hero in "A Peacock Flying Southeast", worked. It happened that the surname of this family was also Jiao, and that the host held a post far away, too. The hostess received Li Bai and the poet thus created the poem "The Hostess of the Lujiang Family". In this poem, Li Bai cited the story of Jiao Zhongqing and Liu Lanzhi to, on the one hand, praise the hostess for her virtues and, on the other, express his mild sorrow for her loneliness. The whole poem is as follows:

Where does the peacock perch
That flies southeast in painful search?

Sewing for the wayfarer that passes by,
The Lujiang official's wife utters a sigh.
Only the city crow caws for thy solitary life,
And away the darkness she tries to drive.

Julie, or the New Heloise

Julie, or the New Heloise, an epistolary novel by Rousseau, is not only a rebellion against feudal patriarchy, but also a hymn to love.

Julie, a young lady of the nobility, fell in love with her tutor St. Preux, but their love affair was strongly opposed by Julie's father due to the huge difference in their social status. Despite the young lovers' struggles, the father still married Julie to Wolmar, a nobleman that was considered a suitable husband for his daughter. St. Preux concealed his love for Julie deeply in his heart and maintained a pure and sincere relationship with Julie and her husband. Julie, at the end of her life, asked St. Preux to take care of her family and marry her cousin Claire. St. Preux agreed to look after Julie's family but refused to marry Claire.

Discussion

1. In that social context, did Liu Lanzhi and Jiao Zhongqing have other choices? Why?
2. Do you know any other literary work that expresses young people's pursuit of freedom and love? Please describe it.

陆　孔雀东南飞

引

《孔雀东南飞》是一首叙事长诗。诗的标题源于用来起兴的诗歌首句。“孔雀东南飞，五里一徘徊”的意象象征着一对年轻夫妇（焦仲卿和刘兰芝）依依不舍的眷恋之情。

这首诗标志着中国古代叙事诗的成熟。以下故事就是根据《玉台新咏》所收录的诗作改编而来的。

◎ 石苇盟约图
刻于安徽省怀宁县孔雀东南飞文化园内的木板上

故事

一只孔雀向东南方飞去，飞上五里就徘徊一阵。

有一天晚上，当在外任职的焦仲卿回来与妻子小聚时，年轻的妻子哭泣道："十三岁到十六岁，我学习了织布、缝衣服、弹箜篌和读经书；十七岁，我成了你的妻子。我每天在织布机前辛辛苦苦工作到深夜，可还是不能让你的母亲满意。请去告诉她，允许我离开吧。"

听说了此事，仲卿的母亲怒不可遏，跟她的儿子说兰芝配不上他。仲卿无可奈何，只好恳求兰芝暂时回娘家。

拂晓，兰芝梳妆完毕，告别婆婆和小姑便上了车。兰芝离开前，仲卿低声说道："等着我，我很快就接你回来。"

"愿你的爱像磐石那样坚定不移，我的爱如蒲苇那样坚韧不折。"兰芝回答道。

听说这个美丽贤淑的年轻女子离婚了，媒人接踵而来。最终，兰芝屈服于兄长的压力，答应嫁给一个官员的儿子。

婚礼场面极其盛大。仲卿匆匆赶来，伤心不已，说道："恭喜啊！磐石仍然坚定不移，可是蒲苇却已失去韧性。祝你幸福。至于我，就让死亡成为我的归宿。"

"请公平一点，仲卿。我们俩都是被迫接受了我们的命运，就让我们在另一个世界团聚吧。"兰芝答道。

黄昏时分，兰芝跃入池塘，而仲卿则自缢于东南方的一棵树上。两家人十分悲痛和后悔，将他们合葬。在那里，松柏梧桐长得郁郁葱葱，树间有两只小鸟，日夜对着彼此歌唱。

◎ 安徽省怀宁县的孔雀台
始建于唐朝，相传为焦刘爱情故事的发生地

文化链接

乐府

乐府原本指古代朝廷建立的音乐机构，负责掌管朝廷使用的音乐，收集百姓创作的民歌。后来，乐府成了一种诗歌体裁。

乐府诗一般是五言句式。《木兰辞》和《孔雀东南飞》被很多人认为是两首最好的乐府诗，被称为“乐府双璧”。

《庐江主人妇》

公元748年，著名的唐代诗人李白路过庐江郡治一户官宦人家。庐江郡治是《孔雀东南飞》的男主人公焦仲卿任职的地方。巧合的是，这户人家也姓焦，男主人也在外任职。女主人接待了李白。于是，李白便作了《庐江主人妇》这首诗。他在诗中引用了焦仲卿和刘兰芝的故事，一方面赞美了女主人的贤惠，另一方面也对她的孤独略表哀伤。整首诗如下：

孔雀东飞何处栖，
庐江小吏仲卿妻。
为客裁缝君自见，
城乌独宿夜空啼。

《新爱洛伊丝》

卢梭所著的书信体小说《新爱洛伊丝》，既是对封建家长制的反抗，也是对爱情的歌颂。

贵族小姐朱莉和她的家庭教师圣普乐相爱，但由于二人社会地位悬殊，他们的恋情遭到了朱莉父亲的强烈反对。尽管这对年轻的恋人苦苦抗争，父亲还是将朱莉嫁给了被认为适合做女儿丈夫的贵族沃尔玛。圣普乐将他对朱莉的爱深深埋在心底，与朱莉夫妇保持着纯洁真诚的关系。临终前，朱莉请求圣普乐照顾她的家人，并与她的表妹克莱尔结婚。圣普乐答应照顾她的家人，却拒绝和克莱尔结婚。

讨论

1. 在当时的社会背景下，刘兰芝和焦仲卿还有其他的选择吗？为什么？
2. 你知道其他表达年轻人追求自由和爱情的文学作品吗？请讲述一下。

VII GAN JIANG AND MO YE

Introduction

Mount Mogan is a well-known summer resort situated in Deqing County of Zhejiang Province. It was named after a couple (Gan Jiang and Mo Ye) living in the Spring and Autumn Period, who forged a unique pair of swords here.

The following story is adapted from *In Search of the Supernatural*.

◉ The Sword Pond at Mount Mogan, said to be where Gan Jiang and Mo Ye forged and polished swords

Story Time

The king of the Chu State ordered Gan Jiang and Mo Ye to forge a sword for him. It took the couple three years to accomplish the task, which intensely irritated the king.

During the three years, the couple forged two fine swords. Before handing one of them to the king, Gan Jiang said to his pregnant wife, "The king will take my life. When our son grows up, tell him the other sword is hidden under the tree."

The king was already unhappy with the delay. Knowing that Gan Jiang and Mo Ye had forged two swords but handed him only one, the king became even angrier and killed Gan Jiang immediately.

Gan Jiang and Mo Ye had a son named Chi. After Chi grew up, he asked his mother, "Mom, where is my father?" Mo Ye told her son the whole story and Chi was determined to avenge his father.

Meanwhile, the king dreamed of Chi attempting to kill him. So he offered a reward for the head of Chi. Indignant and depressed, Chi cried, which aroused the attention of a swordsman.

"Why are you crying so sadly, young man?" asked the swordsman.

"The king of the Chu State killed my father Gan Jiang ... I have to avenge my father," replied Chi.

"I shall help you should you surrender your head and sword to me." Chi did as he instructed. The swordsman promised, "I won't let you down."

The swordsman went to see the king with Chi's head and seized the opportunity to kill the king. He fulfilled his promise.

⊙ A statue of Gan Jiang and Mo Ye forging swords, situated at Mount Mogan in Deqing County of Zhejiang Province

Cultural Links

In Search of the Supernatural

In Search of the Supernatural, compiled by Gan Bao, a historian of the Eastern Jin Dynasty, is a literary work that records stories of gods and monsters. Most stories in the book are short, simple, imaginative and romantic.

In Search of the Supernatural had a big influence on later literary works. Marvel tales of the Tang Dynasty, operas of the Yuan and Ming dynasties, and *Strange Tales from a Chinese Studio* by Pu Songling of the Qing Dynasty were all closely related to this book.

The sword culture in ancient China

The sword, which carries a diverse collection of cultural meanings, is not merely a weapon. It is honored as "the king of weaponry". Throughout history, many men of letters have been keen on swords. For instance, Qu Yuan once "sang while carrying a sword", and Li Bai "was fond of swordsmanship from the age of 15".

It was highly valued by ancient people that a gentleman should have "a *qin*-like heart and sword-like guts". That means a gentleman should be mentally refined as well as intrepid and resolute. The *qin* represents the temperate and courteous aspect of Chinese culture; the sword interprets another aspect of Chinese culture—bravery and fearlessness.

The Chrysanthemum and the Sword

The Chrysanthemum and the Sword was written by American anthropologist Ruth Benedict, and it is an analysis of Japanese culture. The pursuit of beauty and the belief in warriorship, which are reflected in ikebana and sumo respectively, have been coexisting in Japanese culture for a long time. The book uses the chrysanthemum and the sword to explain the duality of Japanese culture, and it gains great popularity in America.

Discussion

1. What personality traits does the swordsman in the story have?

2. What similarities and differences between Chinese and Japanese culture can you see from "a *qin*-like heart and sword-like guts" and "the chrysanthemum and the sword"?

柒　干将和莫邪

引

莫干山是著名的避暑胜地，位于浙江省德清县。莫干山以春秋时期的一对夫妇（干将和莫邪）命名，他们在这儿铸造了一对天下无双的宝剑。

以下故事改编自《搜神记》。

◎ 位于莫干山的剑池
相传为干将、莫邪铸剑磨剑处

故事

楚王让干将和莫邪为他铸剑。夫妻俩花了三年才完成这个任务，这令楚王十分生气。

夫妻俩在这三年里铸就了两把好剑。干将把其中一把交给楚王前，对怀有身孕的妻子说：“楚王会要我的命。等我们的儿子长大了，告诉他另一把剑藏在树下。”

楚王本来就因为延误而不高兴，得知干将和莫邪铸就了两把剑却只交给他一把后，更是恼怒，立刻杀掉了干将。

干将和莫邪的儿子名叫赤。赤长大后，就问自己的母亲：“母亲，我父亲在哪儿呢？”莫邪就对儿子道出原委，赤决定为父报仇。

与此同时，楚王梦见赤想要杀他，因此悬赏赤的人头。赤又愤怒又伤心，就哭了，这引起了一位剑客的注意。

“年轻人，你为何哭得如此伤心？”剑客问道。

“楚王杀了我的父亲干将……我必须为父报仇。”赤回答。

“如果你肯将你的头颅与剑给我的话，我就会帮你。”赤照他说的做了。剑客承诺道：“我不会辜负你的。”

剑客带着赤的头颅去见楚王，并借机杀了楚王。他兑现了自己的承诺。

◎ 干将、莫邪铸剑雕塑
位于浙江省德清县莫干山

文化链接

《搜神记》

《搜神记》，东晋史学家干宝编撰，是一部记录神怪故事的文学著作。书中大多数故事短小简单，富有想象力和浪漫主义色彩。

《搜神记》对后来的文学作品产生了较大的影响，唐代传奇、元明戏曲以及清代蒲松龄的《聊斋志异》，都和这本书有着密切的联系。

中国古代剑文化

剑不单单是武器，也承载着多种文化内涵，被誉为“百兵之君”。历史上许多文人都热衷于剑，比如屈原曾“挟剑而歌”，李白“十五好剑术”。

君子应当有“琴心剑胆”，古人十分看重这一点，意思是君子应该既情致高雅，又英勇果敢。“琴”代表了中华文化温和谦恭的那一面，“剑”则诠释了中华文化的另一面——勇敢无畏。

《菊与剑》

《菊与剑》是美国人类学家鲁思·贝内迪克特的著作，该书剖析了日本文化。尚美与黩武长期并存于日本文化之中，分别反映在花道和相扑上。该书借菊与剑解释了日本文化的双重性，在美国很受欢迎。

讨论

1. 故事中的剑客有什么样的性格特点?
2. 从“琴心剑胆”和“菊与剑”中，你可以看出中日文化有哪些相同之处和不同之处?

VIII THE RECORD OF THE PEACH BLOSSOM SPRING

Introduction

"The Record of the Peach Blossom Spring" is a piece of prose depicting an ideal world where people are isolated from the outside world and lead a peaceful and harmonious life.

It was written by Tao Yuanming, who is said to be the father of Chinese fields and gardens poetry. He was born in the Eastern Jin Dynasty. Tired of life as an official, he resigned his post and lived in seclusion. He spent most of his life living in the countryside: tilling the land, growing crops, reading books, and writing poetry.

The Chinese idiom "the peach blossom spring", which means "an ideal society cut off from the outside world", is derived from the prose "The Record of the Peach Blossom Spring". The following story is adapted from this prose.

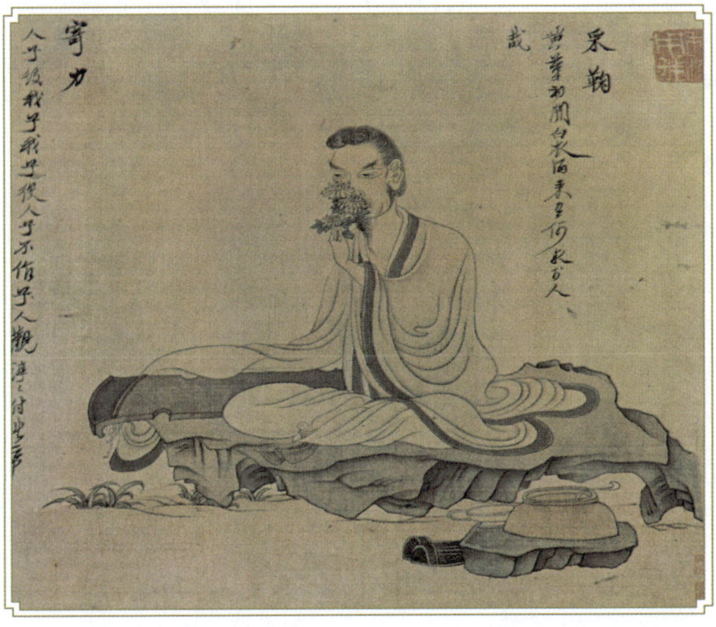

⊙ A portrait of Tao Yuanming, painted by Chen Hongshou of the late Ming Dynasty

Story Time

During the Taiyuan Period of the Jin Dynasty, a fisherman living in Wuling County was rowing his boat along a stream. Being forgetful of the distance he traveled, he suddenly came across a grove of peach trees in blossom. The flowers were fresh and beautiful, and the ground was covered by fallen petals. Amazed by what he saw, the fisherman continued rowing, wishing to explore how far it extended.

The grove ended at the source of the stream, and there the fisherman found a hill. On the hill there was a small opening, through which a light seemed to filter. Thus the fisherman got off his boat and entered the opening. At first it was very narrow, barely allowing a person to pass. But after a few dozen paces, the fisherman found it opened out onto a wide plain, where houses were neatly arranged, paths crisscrossed the fields, cocks were crowing, and dogs were barking. Men and women, dressed like people living outside, were busy with their farm work. All of them, whether old or young, beamed with joy and were happy and pleased with themselves.

When the villagers saw the fisherman, they were greatly surprised and asked where he came from. The fisherman answered honestly. The villagers treated him to a feast with wine and chicken. They told the fisherman that their ancestors, fleeing from the wars during the Qin Dynasty, brought their family and neighbors to this place, never went out again, and became cut off from the outside world. They asked what the present dynasty was. The fisherman discovered that they had never heard of the Han Dynasty, let alone the Wei and Jin dynasties. Several days later, the fisherman took leave of them. The villagers said, "Don't mention this place to outsiders."

After the fisherman came out, he found his boat and went back along the same route, making some marks on the way. Upon reaching the county town, he reported what he had seen and heard of to the procurator, who immediately sent some people to find the place with him. They tried to find it through the marks the fisherman previously made but it was all in vain. They could not find that place again.

Cultural Links

⊙ *Fairyland of Peach Blossoms*, painted by Qiu Ying of the Ming Dynasty

Prose in the Wei and Jin dynasties

The Wei and Jin dynasties are a period of turbulence and intranquility in China's history, during which Chinese literature went through many changes. The prose in this period, while expressing political views, involved more and more personal emotions. In addition, *pianwen* gained full development during this period.

Some of the most celebrated prose writers during this period were Lu Ji, Zhang Hua, Wang Xizhi and Tao Yuanming.

The School of Fields and Gardens Poetry

The School of Fields and Gardens Poetry is an important school of ancient Chinese poetry, and poems in this school often include subject matter like countryside scenery, village life, etc. This school originated from the Eastern Jin Dynasty and flourished in the Tang Dynasty.

Tao Yuanming is one of the most important representatives of this school. Other representatives are Wang Wei, Meng Haoran, Fan Chengda, etc.

Famous quotations from Tao Yuanming

What is there I can do to assuage this mood?

Only enjoy myself drinking my unstrained wine.

(Extracted from "The Ninth Day of the Ninth Month of the Year Yi-Yu")

I pluck chrysanthemums under the eastern hedge,
And gaze afar toward the southern mountains.

(Extracted from the fifth poem in the series of "Drinking Wine")

Long I lived checked by the bars of a cage,
Now I have turned again to nature and freedom.

(Extracted from the first poem in the series of "Returning to the Fields")

Utopia

The term "Utopia" refers to an imagined community or society. It was coined from the Greek words *ou* (which means "not") and *topos* (which means "place") by Thomas More in 1516 and appeared in his book *Utopia*.

In the book, the author depicted a small island in the South Atlantic Ocean, on which there existed perfect systems of politics, economy and law. However, it can be discerned from the literal meaning of the word that a society of this kind did not exist.

Discussion

1. If you were the fisherman in the story, would you mention the peach blossom spring to outsiders? Why?
2. Do you know any other story about Utopia? Please describe it.

捌　桃花源记

引

《桃花源记》是一篇散文，描绘了一个理想世界，那里的人们与世隔绝，过着安宁和乐的生活。

这篇散文的作者是陶渊明，相传他是中国田园诗的始祖。他生于东晋，因厌恶官场生活而辞官隐居，一生中大部分时间都在乡间生活：耕田、种地、读书、写诗。

成语“世外桃源”就源自《桃花源记》这篇散文，意为“与世隔绝的理想社会”。以下故事就是根据这篇散文改编而来的。

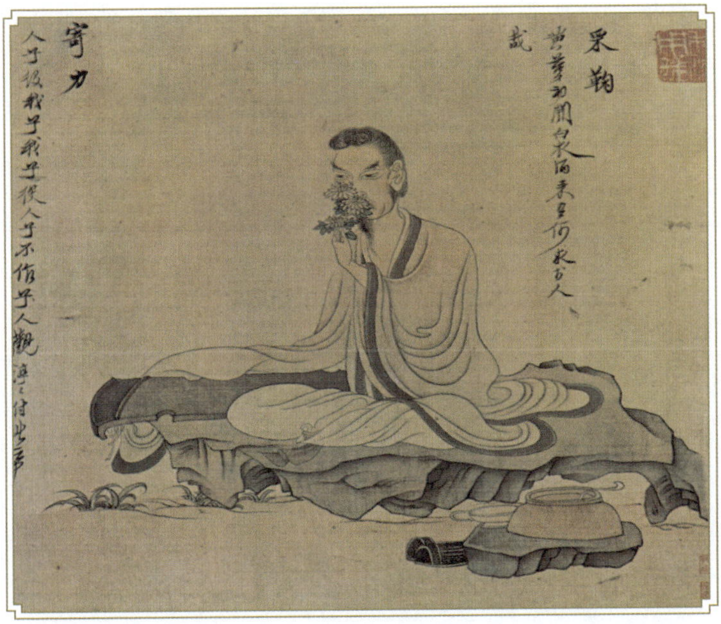

◎ 陶渊明画像
明末陈洪绶绘

故事

晋太元年间，武陵郡有一个渔夫顺着溪水行船。不知走了多远，他忽然看到一片桃花林。花朵鲜嫩美丽，花瓣纷纷散落在地上。渔夫见此情景，感到诧异，就继续划，想探查一下桃花林延伸至多远。

桃花林止于溪水的发源地，渔夫在那里发现了一座山，山上有一个小洞，洞里似乎透出了一点光亮。于是渔夫便下了船，走进洞口。洞口起初非常狭窄，仅容一人通过。但走了几十步后，渔夫发现洞口与一片宽广的平原相接，那里房舍排列整齐，田间小路交错相通，一片鸡鸣狗叫之声。男男女女都在忙于农务，其衣着与在外面生活的人别无二致。所有的人，无论老人还是孩子，都眉开眼笑，怡然自得。

村民看到渔夫，倍感惊诧，问他从何而来。渔夫据实回答。村民备酒杀鸡，设宴款待渔夫。村民告诉渔夫，他们的祖先为了躲避秦代的战争，带着家人和邻居到了这个地方，没有再出去过，跟外界断了联系。村民询问如今是何朝何代，渔夫发现他们竟从未听闻汉朝，遑论魏晋两朝了。过了几日，渔夫向村民告别。村民说：“勿对外人说起此处！”

渔夫出来后，找到他的船，沿原路返回，途中做了一些标记。一到郡城，他便向太守报告了他的所见所闻。太守立即派人跟他去寻找桃花源。他们试图通过渔夫之前所做的标记找到它，但却徒劳无功。他们再也找不到那个地方了。

文化链接

魏晋散文

魏晋两朝是中国历史上动荡不安的一段时期。在这期间，中国文学经历了许多变化。这一时期的散文，在表达政治见解的同时，也夹杂了越来越多的个人情感。此外，在这一时期，骈文得到了较大发展。

这一时期最著名的一些散文家有陆机、张华、王羲之、陶渊明。

田园诗派

田园诗派是中国古代诗歌的一个重要流派，这一流派的诗歌通常涵盖乡间景色、乡村生活等题材。该流派源于东晋，盛于唐朝。

陶渊明是这一诗派最重要的代表人物之一。其他代表人物有王维、孟浩然、范成大等。

陶渊明的名句

何以称我情？浊酒且自陶。（摘自《己酉岁九月九日》）

采菊东篱下，悠然见南山。（摘自《饮酒（其五）》）

久在樊笼里，复得返自然。（摘自《归园田居（其一）》）

◎《桃源仙境图》
明代仇英绘

乌托邦

“乌托邦”这个词指一个虚构的团体或社会。它是托马斯·莫尔于1516年根据希腊词语*ou*（意为“无”）和*topos*（意为“处所”）创造的，出现在托马斯·莫尔的《乌托邦》一书中。

在这本书中，作者描绘了一个位于南大西洋中的小岛，岛上有完美的政治、经济、法律体系。然而，从词的字面意思可见，一个这样的社会并不存在。

讨论

1. 如果你是故事中的渔夫，你会向外人提起桃花源吗？为什么？
2. 你知道其他关于乌托邦的故事吗？请讲述一下。

IX THE OLD CHARCOAL SELLER

Introduction

"The Old Charcoal Seller" is a Tang poem describing the miserable experience of an old charcoal seller. Through the poem, the author criticized the oppression of the lower-class working people by the ruling class and showed deep sympathy toward the poor.

⊙ A portrait of Bai Juyi, painted by Chen Hongshou of the late Ming Dynasty

The author of the poem is Bai Juyi, one of the most renowned poets in the Tang Dynasty. Most of his works were written in popular language and accessible to ordinary people. Apart from "The Old Charcoal Seller", his famous works also include "Song of a Pipa Player" and "The Everlasting Regret".

The following story is adapted from the poem "The Old Charcoal Seller".

Story Time

There lived an old charcoal seller, who cut wood and made charcoal in the mountains all year around. His whole face, covered with dust and ash, had turned to the color of smoke; the hair on his temples had turned grizzled; his fingers had turned black. He scraped along on a meager income from the sale of charcoal. Though his coat was very thin, he still hoped cold days would set in. Thus the charcoal could fetch a good price.

At night, a heavy snow fell outside the city. At dawn, the old man drove his charcoal cart to the market. When he arrived, the sun had risen high. The ox was weary and he was hungry. Outside the southern gate of the market, he stopped to have a rest in the mud.

Suddenly, a pair of arrogant men came on their horses. Who could they be? A palace eunuch in yellow and his attendant in white. With an edict in hand (which the eunuch said was an imperial decree), they pulled the cart and shouted at the ox, heading back to the north.

A cartload of charcoal weighed more than 1,000 catties. Though very loath to let it go, the old man dared not resist. Twenty feet of red silk and 10 feet of damask were tied to the head of the ox as the price of the whole cart of charcoal.

Cultural Links

Tang poetry

Tang poetry generally refers to the poetry written in the Tang Dynasty, which is regarded as the golden age of Chinese poetry. During this period, poetry was an important part of social life and men of letters were required to master poetry writing skills. *Complete Tang Poems*, compiled by Peng Dingqiu and his colleagues, includes more than 49,000 poems.

Tang poems usually have five-character or seven-character lines and consist of multiple rhyming couplets. The most celebrated poets in the Tang Dynasty are Li Bai, Du Fu, Bai Juyi, Wang Wei, etc, and many of their poems still enjoy great popularity today.

Famous quotations from Bai Juyi

On high, we'd be two lovebirds flying wing to wing;
On earth, two trees with branches twined from spring to spring.
(Extracted from "The Everlasting Regret")

Both of us in misfortune go from shore to shore.
Meeting now, need we have known each other before?
(Extracted from "Song of a Pipa Player")

Fire tries to burn them up in vain;

Zhongnanshan Mountains, said to be where the old charcoal seller cut wood and made charcoal

They rise again when spring winds blow.

(Extracted from "Grass on the Ancient Plain—Farewell to a Friend")

The Little Match Girl

"The Little Match Girl" is a fairy tale describing the miserable life of a little girl. She tried to sell matches on a cold New Year's Eve but was eventually frozen to death in the street. The tale deplores the cruelness and mercilessness of the polarized capitalist society and expresses the author's sympathy toward the poor.

"The Little Match Girl" is one of the representative works of Hans Christian Andersen (1805—1875), an eminent Danish writer of fairy tales, plays, novels and poems.

Discussion

1. Why did the old charcoal seller have to sell the whole cart of charcoal to the palace eunuch at an extremely low price?
2. What was it that made the old charcoal seller and the little match girl so miserable?

玖　卖炭翁

引

《卖炭翁》是一首唐诗，描述了一位卖炭老翁的悲惨遭遇。通过这首诗，作者批判了统治阶级对下层劳动人民的压迫，表达了对穷人的深切同情。

该诗的作者是白居易，唐代最著名的诗人之一。他的大多数作品用通俗的语言写成，普通人也能听懂。除《卖炭翁》之外，他的著名作品还有《琵琶行》和《长恨歌》。

以下故事就是根据《卖炭翁》这首诗改编而来的。

◎ 白居易画像
明末陈洪绶绘

故事

有位卖炭的老翁，整年在山中砍柴制炭。他满脸灰尘，面如烟熏，两鬓灰白，十指发黑，靠着卖炭的微薄收入勉强维持生计。尽管他的衣衫非常单薄，他仍希望冷天能持续，这样炭就可以卖个好价钱。

夜里，城外下起了大雪。清晨，老翁驾着炭车去集市。当他到达时，太阳已高高升起。牛困人饥，他就在集市南门外的泥泞中停下来休息一下。

忽然，有两个趾高气扬的人骑着马过来了。他们会是谁呢？是宫内的黄衣太监和他的白衣随从。他们手拿一份敕令（那个太监说那份敕令是圣旨），一边拉着车一边冲牛吆喝，回北边去了。

一车炭有一千多斤。老翁很舍不得炭被拉走，但又不敢反抗。半匹红纱和一丈绫被系在了牛头上，充当了一整车炭的价钱。

文化链接

唐诗

唐诗泛指创作于唐朝的诗。唐朝被认为是中国诗歌的鼎盛时期。在这一时期，诗是社会生活的重要组成部分，文人需要掌握写诗的技巧。彭定求及其同伴汇编的《全唐诗》收录了49,000多首诗。

唐诗通常是五言句式或七言句式，由多个押韵的对句组成。唐代最著名的诗人有李白、杜甫、白居易、王维等。他们的很多诗至今仍脍炙人口。

白居易的名句

在天愿作比翼鸟，在地愿为连理枝。（摘自《长恨歌》）

同是天涯沦落人，相逢何必曾相识。（摘自《琵琶行》）

野火烧不尽，春风吹又生。（摘自《赋得古原草送别》）

《卖火柴的小女孩》

《卖火柴的小女孩》是一个童话故事，讲述了一个小女孩的悲惨生活。她试图在

◎ 终南山
相传为卖炭翁伐薪制炭的地方

寒冷的新年前夜去卖火柴，最终却冻死街头。该故事鞭挞了两极分化的资本主义社会的残酷无情，表达了作者对穷人的同情。

《卖火柴的小女孩》是汉斯·克里斯汀·安徒生（1805—1875）的代表作之一。安徒生是丹麦著名童话作家、剧作家、小说家、诗人。

讨论

1. 为什么卖炭翁不得不将一整车炭以极低的价钱卖给宫内的太监?
2. 是什么使得卖炭翁和卖火柴的小女孩如此悲惨?

X THE GOVERNOR OF NANKE

Introduction

In Yangzhou City of Jiangsu Province, a pagoda tree has been standing silently for over 1,000 years. As early as more than 1,000 years ago, a man's dream made it famous far and wide.

"The Governor of Nanke" recounts the story of Chunyu Fen having a dream under the tree. The Chinese idiom "a Nanke dream" originates from this story and means an empty joy.

The following story is adapted from "The Governor of Nanke".

◎ The thousand-year-old pagoda tree, standing in Yangzhou City of Jiangsu Province

Story Time

Chunyu Fen, an officer in the Tang Dynasty, was dismissed for offending his general. Since then, he drank every day to rid himself of the depression.

One day, he drank himself stupid under a pagoda tree as usual. While he was half-awake, he saw two messengers invite him into a carriage. He did as they asked. The carriage entered the hole in the pagoda tree. He was surprised to find a different world hidden in the hole!

There was nobody but verdant mountains and green waters on the road. The carriage moved forward and finally stopped in front of a grand gate, on which was inscribed "The Great Kingdom of Huai'an".

Chunyu Fen was informed that he was invited here to marry the princess. After the wedding ceremony, Chunyu Fen was appointed as the governor of Nanke County.

In the following 20 years, Chunyu Fen was diligent in government affairs, and Nanke County was in perfect order under his governance. Chunyu Fen was trusted by the king and supported by the people. He had five sons, who all took official posts, and two daughters, who both married into the royal family.

One day, the Kingdom of Tanluo suddenly invaded. Chunyu Fen led troops to fight against the enemy, but suffered one defeat after another. Misfortune never came alone. His wife died of illness at that time. Therefore, he decided to go back to his hometown for a visit. Chunyu Fen got back home, only to find himself lying on the corridor. It turned out that a day had scarcely passed in reality.

Chunyu Fen walked to the pagoda tree and unearthed a huge ant nest. It suddenly dawned on him that the Great Kingdom of Huai'an was just the ant nest!

◎ The mural of *Nanke Dream*, located in the Lü Dongbin Temple in Handan City, Hebei Province

Cultural Links

The marvel tale

"The Governor of Nanke" is a marvel tale, which is one genre of fiction.

A marvel tale generally refers to a short story written in classical Chinese, and it may include subject matter like love, heroes, gods, demons, etc.

Marvel tales of the Tang Dynasty served as a vast reservoir, from which numerous dramas and novels were produced.

A golden millet dream

In the marvel tales of the Tang Dynasty, there is another similar story about dream, which was recorded in "The World Inside a Pillow".

In the story, a poor scholar lived a glorious life in his dream after he got a pillow from the immortal Lü Dongbin. But before the golden millet was well cooked, he woke up from the dream.

Now the Chinese idiom "a golden millet dream" often means a wish that can never be realized; it also indicates that high honor and great wealth are as transient as a fleeting cloud.

The Dream of Akinosuke

"The Dream of Akinosuke" is a Japanese folktale collected in *Kwaidan: Stories and Studies of Strange Things*. It recounts a story about a squire, who saw through life through experiences in his dream.

Kwaidan: Stories and Studies of Strange Things includes some ghost stories written in English as well as a brief study on insects. It was written by Patrick Lafcadio Hearn (his Japanese name is Koizumi Yakumo), who is the founding father of modern Japanese mystery literature.

Discussion

1. What impact would the dream possibly make on Chunyu Fen's future life?

2. Is a dream a reflection of real life? Why?

拾　南柯太守传

引

在江苏省扬州市，一棵槐树已静静伫立了一千多年。早在千年以前，一个人的一个梦，让这棵古树声名远扬。

《南柯太守传》讲述了淳于棼在此树下做梦的故事。成语“南柯一梦”便出自这个故事，指一场空欢喜。

以下故事改编自《南柯太守传》。

◎ 千年槐树
位于江苏省扬州市

故事

淳于棼是唐代一名官员，因冒犯他的主帅而被撤职。此后，他天天借酒消愁。

有一天，他又像往常一样在槐树下喝得晕头转向。半睡半醒时，他看到两名使者邀请他上马车，就按他们说的做了。车驶进了槐树洞口。他惊讶地发现洞里竟别有洞天！

路上没有行人，只有青山绿水。马车向前行驶，最终停在了一扇大门前，上面写着“大槐安国”。

淳于棼被告知，请他过来，是想让他娶公主。婚礼过后，淳于棼被委任为南柯郡太守。

之后二十年，淳于棼勤于政务，将南柯郡治理得井井有条，既获君王器重，又获百姓拥戴。他有五子二女，儿子皆担任官职，女儿皆嫁入了皇族。

有一天，檀萝国突然入侵。淳于棼率兵抗敌，却节节败退。祸不单行，他的妻子在那时病逝了。因此，他决定回乡探访。淳于棼返回家中，只见自己躺在走廊上，原来现实中一日还未过去。

淳于棼朝槐树走去，掘出个很大的蚂蚁洞。他恍然大悟，原来大槐安国正是这个蚂蚁洞啊！

◎《南柯梦》壁画
位于河北省邯郸市吕仙祠

文化链接

传奇

《南柯太守传》是一部传奇，传奇是小说体裁之一。

传奇一般指用文言写成的短篇小说，其题材可能包括爱情、英雄、神灵、鬼怪等。

唐传奇是一个巨大的资料库，许多戏剧、小说据此产生。

黄粱一梦

唐传奇中，有另一则关于梦的相似的故事，载于《枕中记》。

故事中，一个贫穷的书生得到仙人吕洞宾给他的枕头后，在睡梦中度过了荣耀的一生。然而，小米饭还没煮熟，他就从梦中醒来了。

现在，“黄粱一梦”这个成语通常指不能实现的愿望，也指荣华富贵如过眼云烟。

《安艺之介梦游记》

《安艺之介梦游记》是一个日本民间故事，收编于《怪谈》。它讲述了一位乡绅通过睡梦中的经历看透人生的故事。

《怪谈》包括一些用英文写成的鬼怪故事，以及一项对昆虫的简单研究，其作者是日本现代怪谈文学的鼻祖帕特里克·拉夫卡迪奥·赫恩（他的日本姓名是小泉八云）。

讨论

1. 那场梦可能对淳于棼未来的生活产生什么影响?

2. 梦是对现实生活的反映吗?为什么?

XI COMPOSING STIRRING WORDS FOR CHEN TONGFU

Introduction

Xin Qiji was a poet and military leader of the Southern Song Dynasty, who expressed his concern for the nation in his poetry.

Xin's poetry, diversified in style, spans a great range of subject matter. The poet is adept at using allusions. His works, most of which are in the *haofang* style, are not limited to one type. Xin Qiji and Su Shi are collectively called "Su Xin" while Xin Qiji and Li Qingzhao are collectively known as "Two Ans from Ji'nan" (both poets were born in Ji'nan, and their courtesy names are You'an and Yi'an respectively).

Xin lived in seclusion in the mountains after being dismissed from service. It was during this period that he met a like-minded friend, Chen Tongfu. The following story is adapted from Xin's work "*Pozhenzi*—Composing Stirring Words for Chen Tongfu", which was composed after Xin and Chen's meeting at the Goose Lake.

◉ The Goose Lake Academy, constructed to commemorate Xin Qiji and Chen Tongfu's Goose Lake meeting, located in Shangrao City of Jiangxi Province

Story Time

This was another drunken night. Getting a bit tipsy, I raised the wick to make the lamp brighter. In the flickering light, I drew out my dearest sword and looked at it again and again.

Having drifted off to sleep, I went back to the battlefield in my dream. From tent to tent, the bugles resounded. I shared grilled beef with my subordinates. Military melodies were played loudly on various musical instruments, which aroused the soldiers' patriotic sentiment. The autumn sky was clear and the air was bracing. A parade of soldiers had already assembled on the field, ready to be inspected.

Steeds galloped across the field, stirring clouds of dust. It reminded me of the story of Liu Bei and his steed Dilu, who helped his master free from the enemy running after them. At that time, Dilu got stuck in the water and Liu Bei anxiously said, "Dilu, come on … or we'll lose our lives today!" Hearing these words, Dilu jumped high and galloped away, just like today's war horses.

With their bows at full draw, the soldiers discharged the arrows at the same time, causing rolls of thunder. I had been fighting bravely, aspiring to recover the lost land for the emperor as well as win everlasting fame for myself.

All of a sudden, I woke up from my dream. In the mirror, I saw a lonely figure with grey hair on his temples. I could do nothing but utter a deep sigh, for the deplorable fate of us and of our nation!

◉ A stamp related to Xin Qiji and his work (*Pozhenzi*—Composing Stirring Words for Chen Tongfu), issued by China Post in 2012

Cultural Links

Ci

Ci, also called "lines of irregular lengths", is a literature form prevalent in the Song Dynasty. Originating in the Sui and Tang dynasties, it reached its zenith in the Song Dynasty. The end of the Ming Dynasty and the beginning of the Qing Dynasty witnessed a revival of *ci* poetry.

The *ci* poetry of the Song Dynasty is comparable to Tang poetry and Yuan opera. In terms of style, it can generally be divided into *wanyue* and *haofang* types. The former is represented by Li Qingzhao, Liu Yong, Qin Guan, etc while the latter is represented by Su Shi, Xin Qiji, etc.

Cipai

Cipai is the name of the formation of *ci*, and it usually consists of three Chinese characters, such as *pozhenzi*. The literal meaning of *cipai* can be rather obscure. Some names come from folk songs such as *dielianhua*, some are introduced from other regions like *pusaman*, and some are taken straight from earlier poems like *yijiangnan*.

Xiaoling, zhongdiao and *changdiao*

According to the number of characters, *ci* can be divided into *xiaoling*, *zhongdiao* and *changdiao*. *Xiaoling* is limited to 58 characters, so *dianjiangchun* and *huanxisha* belong to this type. A *ci* poem that contains 59—90 characters is called *zhongdiao*, such as *yijianmei* and *pozhenzi*. *Changdiao*, like *niannujiao* and *hexinlang*, contains more than 90 characters.

The Eve of Waterloo

"The Eve of Waterloo" is a poem written by British poet George Gordon Byron, depicting the scene before the outbreak of the Battle of Waterloo. The following is part of the poem.

And there was mounting in hot haste: the steed,
The mustering squadron, and the clattering car,
Went pouring forward with impetuous speed,

And swiftly forming in the ranks of war;
And the deep thunder peal on peal afar;
And near, the beat of the alarming drum
Roused up the soldier ere the morning star;
While throng'd the citizens with terror dumb,
Or whispering with white lips—"the foe! They come! They come!"

Discussion

1. What feelings are conveyed in Xin Qiji's work "*Pozhenzi*—Composing Stirring Words for Chen Tongfu"?
2. What are the similarities and differences between Xin Qiji and Byron in their description of war?

拾壹　为陈同甫赋壮语以寄

引

辛弃疾是南宋词人、将领，他把对国家的关切寄托于词作之中。

辛弃疾的词风格多样，题材广阔。诗人善于使用典故。他的作品大部分属于豪放派，但又不拘一格。辛弃疾与苏轼合称“苏辛”，与李清照并称“济南二安”（二人都出生于济南，号分别为幼安和易安）。

辛弃疾被罢官后隐居山中。正是在这段时间，他遇到了与他志同道合的朋友陈同甫。以下故事改编自辛弃疾的作品《破阵子·为陈同甫赋壮语以寄》，这首词创作于辛陈鹅湖聚会之后。

◎ 鹅湖书院
为纪念辛弃疾和陈同甫鹅湖之会而建
位于江西省上饶市

故事

这又是一个醉酒的夜晚。带着几分醉意，我挑亮灯火。灯光摇曳，我拔出最心爱的宝剑，一遍又一遍地端详着它。

我渐渐入眠，在梦中回到了沙场，号角声在一个又一个军营中回荡。我将烤熟的牛肉与部下分享。各种乐器奏起响亮的军乐，这激起了士兵们的爱国热忱。秋高气爽，一队士兵已在沙场集结完毕，等待检阅。

沙场上，战马奔驰，扬起滚滚尘土。我想起了刘备和他的战马的卢的故事。的卢帮助他的主人逃脱了敌军的追捕。那时候，的卢陷入水中，刘备急道：“的卢，努力啊……否则我们今日性命不保！”听到这些话后，的卢高高跃起，驰骋而去，正如今天的这些战马一般。

弓已拉满，士兵们同时将箭射了出去，声如霹雳。一直以来，我英勇作战，渴望替君主收复失地，也为自己赢得永久的美名。

突然，我从梦中醒来。在镜子中，我看到一个孤独的、两鬓斑白的身影。我什么也做不了，只能长叹一声，为我们自己可悲的命运而叹，也为我们民族可悲的命运而叹啊！

◎ 一枚关于辛弃疾和他的作品（《破阵子·为陈同甫赋壮语以寄》）的邮票
2012年由中国邮政发行

文化链接

词

词，也叫长短句，是盛行于宋朝的一种文学形式。词萌芽于隋唐之际，至宋代达到顶峰。明末清初见证了词的复兴。

宋词可与唐诗、元曲比肩。从风格看，宋词通常分为婉约派和豪放派，前者代表人物为李清照、柳永、秦观等，后者代表人物为苏轼、辛弃疾等。

词牌

词牌是词的组织形式的名称，通常由三个汉字构成，比如“破阵子”。词牌的字面意思可能很模糊。有些名字来自民间乐曲，比如“蝶恋花”；有些是从别的地区引入的，比如“菩萨蛮”；还有一些直接取自早期的诗歌，比如“忆江南”。

小令、中调、长调

词根据字数可以分为小令、中调和长调。小令在五十八个字以内，因而“点绛唇”和“浣溪沙”都属于这类。介于五十九个字和九十个字之间的词被称作中调，比如“一剪梅”和“破阵子”。长调超过九十个字，比如“念奴娇”和“贺新郎”。

《滑铁卢前夜》

《滑铁卢前夜》是英国诗人乔治·戈登·拜伦所写的一首诗，描绘了滑铁卢之战爆发之前的情景。以下是这首诗的部分内容。

> 到处是急急匆匆的上马：战马，
> 集合的骑队，炮车震响个不停，
> 纷纷都火急飞快地向战地出发，
> 顷刻间一排排都列成作战的队形；
> 远处是一阵又一阵深沉的雷鸣；

近处是报警的铜鼓一齐打开了，
不等到启明星隐退就催起所有的士兵；
老百姓挤在一起，都给吓呆了，
或者战战兢兢悄悄说——“敌人来了，来了！”

讨论

1. 辛弃疾的作品《破阵子 · 为陈同甫赋壮语以寄》传达了什么样的情感？
2. 辛弃疾和拜伦对战争的描述有什么相同之处和不同之处？

XII THE INJUSTICE TO DOU E

Introduction

The surface of Mercury is covered with a large number of craters, some of which have been named by the International Astronomical Union (IAU) after world-famous writers, artists and composers. So far, some Mercurian craters have been named after Chinese notables, among whom there are two famous playwrights in the Yuan Dynasty—Guan Hanqing and Ma Zhiyuan.

Guan Hanqing, Ma Zhiyuan, Zheng Guangzu and Bai Pu, whose works represented the great achievements of *zaju* in different periods of the Yuan Dynasty, are collectively known as "Four Great Masters of Yuan Opera".

The Injustice to Dou E, from which the following story is adapted, is one of the masterpieces of Guan Hanqing.

⊙ A stamp commemorating Guan Hanqing, issued by Soviet Postal Service in 1958

Story Time

Dou E was sold to the Cai family as a child bride at the age of seven because her father was unable to repay his debts. At 19, her husband died. Since then, she lived with her widowed mother-in-law.

One day, two villains, Donkey Zhang and his father, happened to save the mother-in-law's life. Learning that both the old woman and her daughter-in-law were widowed, the father and the son broke into the Cai's house and dwelt there. Donkey Zhang tried to force Dou E into marrying him, but Dou E firmly refused, which totally irritated him.

Thus, Donkey Zhang secretly put some poison in the soup that Dou E prepared for her sick mother-in-law. The soup was mistakenly drunk by Donkey Zhang's father, who died within a few minutes.

Seeing this, Donkey Zhang asked Dou E, "What would you like to do? To settle it officially or privately? "

"What do you mean by officially and by privately?" asked Dou E.

"By officially, I mean that you will be arrested on a charge of murder; by privately, I mean I will take no further action if you marry me," replied Donkey Zhang.

Dou E said, "A good horse will not be equipped with two saddles; nor will a chaste woman serve two husbands."

Both Dou E and her mother-in-law were arrested and they suffered various tortures. To free her mother-in-law from the torment, Dou E finally admitted to the killing and was sentenced to death. Before execution, Dou E made three vows. She said, "After my death, my blood will splash onto the white silk but will not drip onto the ground; there will be heavy snowfall in the sixth lunar month and the thick snow will cover my dead body; Chuzhou will experience three years of severe drought."

After Dou E's death, all three events occured, proving her innocence.

◎ *The Injustice to Dou E,* painted on the Long Corridor of the Summer Palace in Beijing

Cultural Links

Zaju

Zaju is a form of Chinese opera and gained great popularity in the Yuan Dynasty. The "Four Great Tragedies" of the Yuan *zaju* include *The Injustice to Dou E* by Guan Hanqing, *Autumn in the Han Palace* by Ma Zhiyuan, *Rain on the Paulownia Tree* by Bai Pu and *The Orphan of Zhao* by Ji Junxiang.

Sanqu

Sanqu is a subtype of *qu*. It resembles the *ci* poetry of the Song Dynasty in that they are both written according to certain metrical forms, but they differ in that *sanqu* is more colloquial. *Sanqu* can be further divided into *xiaoling* and *santao*, and the latter usually contains several melodies.

Ma Zhiyuan's *sanqu* "*Tianjingsha*—Autumn Thoughts" is credited as "the progenitor of autumn thoughts". The whole *sanqu* is as follows:

Over old trees wreathed with rotten vines fly evening crows;
Under a small bridge near a cottage a stream flows;
On an ancient road in the west wind a lean horse goes.
Westward declines the sun;
Far, far from home is the heartbroken one.

Hamlet

Hamlet is a tragedy written by Shakespeare, and the hero is Prince Hamlet.

Claudius, Hamlet's uncle, murdered his own brother, seized the throne, and married his deceased brother's widow. Hamlet was called on by the ghost of his father to take revenge on his uncle.

Hamlet is Shakespeare's longest play, and is considered to be one of the most influential works in the history of world literature.

◎ Kronborg Castle, also known as "Hamlet Castle" as it is the prototype of the Elsinore Castle in *Hamlet*, located in Helsinger, Denmark

Discussion

1. What specific factors led to Dou E's tragedy?
2. What are the similarities and differences between the two characters Dou E and Hamlet?

拾贰　窦娥冤

引

水星表面被很多环形山所覆盖，其中一些已由国际天文学联合会以世界知名的作家、艺术家和作曲家命名。迄今为止，已有一些水星上的环形山以中国的名人来命名，其中包括元代两位著名的戏剧家——关汉卿和马致远。

关汉卿、马致远、郑光祖和白朴并称“元曲四大家”。他们的作品代表了元代不同时期杂剧的突出成就。

《窦娥冤》是关汉卿的代表作之一，以下故事即改编于此。

⊙ 一枚纪念关汉卿的邮票
1958年由苏联邮政发行

故事

窦娥七岁时，由于父亲无法偿还债务，被卖到蔡家当童养媳。十九岁时，她的丈夫去世了。从那以后，她就和守寡的婆婆住在一起。

有一天，两个恶棍，张驴儿和他的父亲，碰巧救了窦娥婆婆一命。父子二人得知婆媳二人均守寡，就闯入蔡家并在那里住了下来。张驴儿试图强迫窦娥与他成亲，但窦娥坚定地拒绝了，这彻底惹恼了他。

于是，张驴儿偷偷在窦娥为生病的婆婆准备的汤里下了毒。汤被张驴儿的父亲误服，他几分钟内就死了。

见此情形，张驴儿问窦娥：“你打算怎么办？官了还是私了？”

窦娥问：“何为官了？何为私了？”

张驴儿答道：“官了的话，你将以谋杀罪被捕；私了的话，你嫁给我，我便不再追究。”

窦娥说：“好马不配双鞍，烈女不侍二夫。”

窦娥和她的婆婆都被捕了，她们遭受了各种酷刑。为了让婆婆免遭折磨，窦娥最终承认杀了人，被判死刑。行刑前，窦娥发下三桩誓愿。她说：“我死后，我的鲜血将溅在白练上而不沾地；六月将下起大雪，大雪将遮盖我的尸体；楚州将大旱三年。”

窦娥死后，三桩事件都发生了，证明了她的清白。

《窦娥冤》
北京颐和园长廊画作

文化链接

杂剧

杂剧是中国戏曲形式的一种，盛行于元代。元杂剧的“四大悲剧”包括关汉卿的《窦娥冤》、马致远的《汉宫秋》、白朴的《梧桐雨》以及纪君祥的《赵氏孤儿》。

散曲

散曲是曲的一种。它与宋词相似，二者都是根据一定的韵律格式填写，但不同的是，散曲更加口语化。散曲可进一步分为小令和散套，后者通常由若干曲子组成。

马致远的散曲《天净沙·秋思》被誉为“秋思之祖”。整首散曲如下：

枯藤老树昏鸦，
小桥流水人家，
古道西风瘦马。
夕阳西下，
断肠人在天涯。

《哈姆雷特》

《哈姆雷特》是莎士比亚所写的一部悲剧。主人公是哈姆雷特王子。

哈姆雷特的叔叔克劳狄斯杀害了自己的兄长，篡取了王位，并娶了兄长的遗孀。父亲的魂魄召唤哈姆雷特向自己的叔叔复仇。

《哈姆雷特》是莎士比亚最长的一部戏剧，被认为是世界文学史上最有影响力的作品之一。

◎ 卡隆堡宫，因为是《哈姆雷特》中埃尔西诺城堡的原型而又被称为“哈姆雷特城堡”位于丹麦赫尔辛格

讨论

1. 什么具体因素造成了窦娥的悲剧？

2. 哈姆雷特和窦娥这两个角色有什么相同之处和不同之处？

XIII LU TIXIA PUNCHING OFFICIAL GUANXI

Introduction

In the novel *Water Margin*, Lu Tixia was a title of Lu Da when he was an official "Tixia". He, who uprooted a weeping willow, was born with surprising strength as well as profound wisdom (which was the cause of his dharma name "Zhishen"). During his lifetime, he had a strong sense of justice and was always ready to help the weak. The literary critic Jin Shengtan praised him as "the best of the best" among the 108 Liangshan heroes.

The following story is adapted from the third chapter of *Water Margin*.

⊙ *Lu Zhishen Uprooting a Weeping Willow*, painted on the Long Corridor of Zhongshan Park in Beijing

Story Time

When Lu Da and his two friends were drinking, they overheard a girl crying over her hardship.

She was Jin Cuilian. A man named Butcher Zheng, who called himself "Official Guanxi", paid for her mother's funeral expenses and deceived her into being his concubine. However, Butcher Zheng's overbearing wife kicked Cuilian out. Butcher Zheng felt he suffered a huge loss so he forced Cuilian to pay the high-interest-rate debt. Hearing this, Lu Da gave Cuilian and her father some money and helped them leave safely.

Lu Da then came to Butcher Zheng's stall, ordering him to cut 10 catties of lean meat without any fat meat and another 10 catties of fat meat without any lean meat. Butcher Zheng carefully cut the meat for the whole morning and wrapped it into two packets. "I still want a packet of gristle without any meat on it," said Lu Da.

"My Tixia, are you kidding me?" "Yes, I am!" Lu Da responded, throwing two packets of meat on Butcher Zheng's face. Butcher Zheng felt flames of anger running from his feet to his head. He grabled a sharp knife on the counter and leaped forward. Lu Da grasped Butcher Zheng's left hand and kicked him on the lower belly.

Butcher Zheng was knocked down. Lu Da stepped on his chest, raised the fist that was as big as a bowl, and hit him. "How dare you call yourself 'Official Guanxi'? How dare you use power and influence to cheat Jin Cuilian?" As Lu Da spoke these words, he punched Butcher Zheng again, who could not take the beating and lost his life.

"How could three blows kill him?! I will be put into jail, and no one will bring me meals," thought Lu Da. He quickly ran away, disappearing like a puff of smoke.

Cultural Links

⊙ *Lu Zhishen Punching "Official Guanxi"*, carved on the window lattice of the Chen Clan Temple in Guangzhou City of Guangdong Province

Water Margin

Water Margin is one of China's "Four Great Classical Novels", and it is said to be written by Shi Nai'an of the late Yuan and early Ming dynasties. The book mainly tells the stories of 108 heroes, who formed an army at Liangshan Marsh and resisted oppression.

Water Margin is an early masterpiece of China's vernacular fiction. With vivid, humorous and colloquial language, the book is especially noted for its excellent characterization, such as the tolerant but not submissive Song Jiang, the true-blue Li Kui, the intrepid Wu Song, and the super-clever Wu Yong. The uniquely featured Liangshan heroes, who enjoy great popularity among Chinese people, jointly construct a classic group image in the history of Chinese literature.

The Chinese chivalry culture

Water Margin is a representative work describing chivalrous heroes.

At the core of the chivalry spirit is righteousness, which may be either at the national level or at the individual level. Chivalrous heroes are often well versed in both polite letters and martial arts; they think highly of moral integrity and independent personality.

The Chinese chivalry culture, formed in the long and profound cultural tradition, manifests people's strong desire for a just society and happy life.

Robin Hood

In English folklore, Robin Hood is a hero. He is a highly skilled archer and swordsman, and is quick-witted and brave. Also, he feels great enmity toward officials and churchmen, and robs the rich and assists the poor. In England, Robin Hood is highly revered by people.

Discussion

1. Do you like the character Lu Da? Why?
2. What are the similarities between Lu Da and Robin Hood?

拾叁　鲁提辖拳打镇关西

引

小说《水浒传》中，鲁提辖是鲁达担任官员“提辖”时的称呼。他倒拔垂杨柳，天生神力，又深具慧根（这也是法号“智深”的由来）。他一生具有强烈的正义感，并且总是乐于帮助弱者。文学评论家金圣叹称赞他是一百零八位梁山好汉中的“上上人物”。

以下故事改编自《水浒传》第三回。

◎《鲁智深倒拔垂杨柳》
北京中山公园长廊画作

故事

鲁达和他的两个朋友正喝着酒，他们无意间听到一名女子哭诉自己的难处。

她是金翠莲。有个叫郑屠的人，自称“镇关西”，付了她母亲的安葬费，骗她做妾。然而，郑屠的悍妻却将翠莲赶了出去。郑屠自觉亏大，便逼迫翠莲偿还高利贷。听到这个情况后，鲁达便给了翠莲父女一些钱，并帮助他们安全离开。

随后，鲁达来到郑屠店中，命他切十斤不见半点肥肉的精肉和十斤没有一点精肉的肥肉。郑屠仔细切了一上午肉，并将其包成两包。“我还要一包软骨，不能有一点肉在上头。”鲁达说。

“我的提辖大人，您莫不是在消遣我？”“正是！”鲁达回答道，同时将两包肉扔到了郑屠的脸上。郑屠感到怒火从脚底直冲头顶，他抓起案上的尖刀，跳了出来。鲁达抓住郑屠的左手，往他的小腹上踢了一脚。

郑屠被击倒了。鲁达踩着他的胸脯，提起碗一样大的拳头朝他砸去。“你也敢称自己是‘镇关西’！你也敢用权势骗得金翠莲！”鲁达说这些话的时候，又打了郑屠一拳。郑屠扛不住打，丢了性命。

“三拳竟打死了他？！我要被送进监狱了，而且没人给我送饭。”鲁达想着，赶紧跑了，像一阵烟一样消失了。

文化链接

《鲁智深拳打镇关西》
刻于广东省广州市陈家祠的窗棂上

《水浒传》

《水浒传》是中国“古典长篇小说四大名著”之一，相传为元末明初的施耐庵所著。该书主要讲述了一百零八位好汉的故事。他们在梁山泊组成军队，反抗欺压。

《水浒传》是中国早期白话小说的杰作。该书语言生动、幽默、口语化，尤以出色的人物塑造而闻名，比如隐忍却并非逆来顺受的宋江、赤胆忠心的李逵、勇敢无畏的武松、机智过人的吴用。梁山英雄独具特色，深入人心，共同构成了中国文学史上的经典人物群像。

中国的侠文化

《水浒传》是描写侠客的代表作。

侠精神的核心是“义”，可能是国家层面的“义”，也可能是个人层面的“义”。侠客通常文武双全，重气节，重视人格的独立。

中国的侠文化从久远深厚的文化传统中孕育而来，体现了人们对公正社会和幸福生活的强烈向往。

罗宾汉

在英国的民间传说中，罗宾汉是一个英雄。他精于箭术和剑术，机智勇敢，还仇视官吏和教士，劫富济贫。在英国，罗宾汉深受人们尊敬。

讨论

1. 你喜欢鲁达这个人物吗？为什么？

2. 鲁达和罗宾汉有什么相似之处？

XIV THE REAL AND THE FAKE MONKEY KING

Introduction

Xuanzang was a Buddhist monk as well as a translator and scholar in the Tang Dynasty. He first traveled around China, gathering sacred Buddhist books, but later was concerned that the Buddhist texts found in China might be incomplete and misinterpreted. So, he decided to go to ancient India to get the sacred scripture.

The story of Xuanzang seeking the sacred scripture inspired a writer of the Ming Dynasty to author a great book, *Journey to the West*. The four heroes of this book have become household characters today.

The following story is adapted from *Journey to the West*.

⊙ A portrait of Xuanzang, found in the Mogao Caves in Dunhuang City of Gansu Province

Story Time

Sun Wukong defeated various monsters during the journey. Again, he killed a few bandits this time. Being furious with the killing, Sanzang recited the band-tightening spell and sent the monkey away despite Wukong's repeated pleading.

In depression and despair, Wukong came to Potaraka in the Southern Ocean, confiding his sorrow and grievance to Bodhisattva Guanyin.

Meanwhile, another monkey, in the disguise of Wukong, approached Sanzang. The monkey stunned Sanzang and snatched the luggage. Wujing returned a while later. Hearing what had happened, he set out for the Mountain of Flowers and Fruit, where he found an arrogant Wukong. Wujing was humiliated but he was unable to counterattack. He had no choice but to turn to Guanyin for help.

Knowing that there must be something wrong, Guanyin sent Wukong and Wujing to the Mountain of Flowers and Fruit to find out the truth. When they arrived, Wukong, to his great astonishment, found another Monkey King, who was identical to him, playing and making merry with crowds of monkeys.

Wukong brandished his cudgel toward the false Monkey King, who turned out to be very powerful, too. They fought and fought, and finally came to the Southern Ocean. They pled with Bodhisattva Guanyin to distinguish the true one from the imposter.

No matter what Guanyin said or did, the two monkeys behaved in the same way. Guanyin could not tell them apart. Then they found Jade Emperor, whose magic mirror did not work on the false monkey. After that, they found King of Hell, who also failed to distinguish one from the other.

Finally, both monkeys stood beneath the lotus throne of Tathagata, who identified the imposter as a six-eared monkey. Everything being clear, Wukong rejoined his master and escorted him to the west to get the sacred scripture.

⊙ *The Real and the Fake Monkey King*, painted on the Long Corridor of Zhongshan Park in Beijing

Cultural Links

Journey to the West

Journey to the West, one of China's "Four Great Classical Novels", is said to be authored by Wu Cheng'en of the Ming Dynasty. It depicts Tang Sanzang's journey to the west to obtain the sacred scripture. The stories are greatly enriched by the participation of Sanzang's three disciples (Wukong, Bajie and Wujing). After 81 ordeals, the four finally obtained the sacred scripture and became Buddhas.

Jianzhen's visits to Japan

The Tang Dynasty is a period of frequent cultural exchange, not only absorbing foreign culture, but also spreading its culture to the outside. Xuanzang went through various ordeals to obtain the sacred scripture from ancient India, while Jianzhen, another Buddhist monk in the Tang Dynasty, made every effort to bring Buddhism to Japan.

Jianzhen made six attempts to visit Japan and finally succeeded on his sixth attempt. He established the Tōshōdai Temple in Nara. Jianzhen lost his eyesight due to the hardships of the journeys.

⊙ The Tōshōdai Temple, situated in Nara, Japan

The Pilgrim's Progress

The Pilgrim's Progress, one of the most influential works of religious English literature, was written by John Bunyan and was published in 1678. Just like *Journey to the West*, this book also tells stories about heroes' going through hardships to eventually arrive at the destination. Both novels praise the heroes' intrepidity and persistence.

Discussion

1. Why did Wukong rejoin his master? Why did Sanzang accept him again?
2. If you were Jianzhen, what forms of culture would you like to introduce from or to Japan? Why?

拾肆　真假美猴王

引

玄奘是唐代僧人、译者及学者。他最初云游中国，收集佛教圣书，后来担心在中国找到的佛经或许不够完整或有误读之处，因而决定去天竺取经。

玄奘取经的故事给一位明代作家带来了灵感，他写了一部巨著，即《西游记》。书中的四位主人公如今已成为家喻户晓的人物。

以下故事改编自《西游记》。

◎ 玄奘画像
发现于甘肃省敦煌市的莫高窟

故事

孙悟空一路击退了各种妖怪，这次又杀了几个强盗。三藏怒其杀生，尽管悟空百般哀求，他还是念紧箍咒将悟空赶走了。

悟空感到伤心绝望，便来到南海珞珈山，向观音菩萨诉说自己的懊丧和委屈。

与此同时，另一只猴子化作悟空模样，来到三藏身旁。他将三藏打昏，抢走了包袱。过了一会儿，悟净回来了。听了所发生的事之后，悟净便前往花果山。在那里，他找到了傲慢自大的悟空。悟净受到了羞辱，却无力还击。他别无选择，只得去找观音求助。

观音知道定有蹊跷，便派悟空和悟净去花果山一探究竟。他们到达水帘洞时，悟空大吃一惊，发现有一个与自己一模一样的美猴王正与众猴嬉戏作乐。

悟空挥起他的金箍棒就朝假美猴王打去，事实证明假美猴王也很厉害。他们打来打去，最后来到了南海，请求观音菩萨一辨真假。

无论观音说什么或做什么，两只猴子表现得一模一样。观音不能区分二者。然后，他们找到玉皇大帝，玉帝的照妖镜也照不出假美猴王。之后，他们找到阎罗王，阎罗王也分辨不出谁是谁。

最终，两只猴子站到了如来佛的莲花宝座下面。佛祖识得假悟空是一只六耳猕猴。真相大白，悟空又回到师父身边，护送师父去西天取经。

《真假美猴王》
北京中山公园长廊画作

文化链接

《西游记》

《西游记》是中国“古典长篇小说四大名著”之一，相传由明代吴承恩所著。该书讲述了唐三藏到西天取经的历程。三藏的三位徒弟（悟空、八戒、悟净）的加入，大大丰富了故事内容。经历了八十一难之后，他们四人终于取得真经，修成正果。

鉴真东渡日本

唐代是一个文化交流频繁的时代，不仅吸收外来文化，同时也将它的文化向外传播。玄奘历经种种磨难从天竺取得经书，而另一个唐代僧人鉴真则不遗余力地把佛教传到日本。

鉴真六次尝试东渡日本，最终在第六次尝试时获得成功。他在奈良建立了唐招提寺。由于旅途艰辛，鉴真双目失明。

◎ 唐招提寺
位于日本奈良

《天路历程》

《天路历程》是英国宗教文学中最有影响力的著作之一，出版于1678年，作者是约翰·班扬。和《西游记》类似，该书也讲述了主人公历尽艰难险阻最终到达目的地的故事。两部小说都赞颂了主人公的无所畏惧和坚持不懈。

讨论

1. 悟空为何会回到师父身边？三藏为何再次接受他？
2. 如果你是鉴真，你会从日本引进或向其输出什么形式的文化？为什么？

XV BROTHERHOOD FORGED IN THE PEACH GARDEN

Introduction

The widespread poem "*Linjiangxian*—O So Vast, O So Mighty, the Great River Rolls to Sea" was composed by Yang Shen of the Ming Dynasty, and was later taken by Luo Guanzhong as a prologue to *Romance of the Three Kingdoms*. It is an aria for the eternal universe and for the transient heroes as well. The whole poem is as follows:

O so vast, O so mighty,
The Great River rolls to sea,
Flowers do waves thrash,
Heroes do sands smash,
When all the dreams drain,
Same are loss and gain.

Green mountains remain,
Under pink sunsets,
Hoary fishers and woodcutters,
Along the banks, find calm water,
In autumn moon or in spring wind,
By the wine jars, fill porcelain.

Discuss talk and tale,
Only laugh and gale.

The following story is adapted from *Romance of the Three Kingdoms*.

⊙ An illustration from *Romance of the Three Kingdoms*, depicting Liu, Guan and Zhang swearing brotherhood in the peach garden

Story Time

At the end of the Eastern Han Dynasty, there were flames of war raging everywhere. The court issued an edict to recruit soldiers, which immediately attracted a hero's attention. He was Liu Bei, who was earning a living by selling straw sandals.

Liu Bei uttered a long sigh at the sight of the notice. Suddenly he heard a voice behind him, as loud as thunder. "Why are you sighing instead of devoting yourself to the country?"

Turning around, Liu Bei immediately realized the man was not an ordinary person. He was Zhang Fei, to whom Liu Bei introduced himself: "Liu Bei is my name. I have been dreaming of pacifying the world, but that's beyond my power."

"I've got a small fortune," said Zhang Fei. "What about doing a great deed together?" Liu Bei was very glad and the two went to an inn to talk about their great plan.

As they were drinking, a fellow entered. With a huge build, a long beard and a crimson face, the man was awe-inspiring. This was Guan Yu, who joined Liu and Zhang soon. The three men talked for a long time, finding their ambitions and interests were much the same. Finally, they decided to swear brotherhood.

The next day, they went to Zhang Fei's farm. At this time, the peach trees were in full bloom and the incense was curling upward. The three made a pledge: "Liu Bei, Guan Yu and Zhang Fei, in spite of different families, swear brotherhood here. From now on, we promise to work together with one heart, protecting the country and safeguarding the people. Though not born on the same day, we seek to die together."

Of the trio, Liu Bei was the elder brother, Guan Yu the middle and Zhang Fei the youngest.

◉ *Swearing Brotherhood*, painted on the Long Corridor of Zhongshan Park in Beijing

Cultural Links

Romance of the Three Kingdoms

Romance of the Three Kingdoms is one of China's "Four Great Classical Novels", and it was written by Luo Guanzhong of the late Yuan and early Ming dynasties.

Romance of the Three Kingdoms displays a historical picture scroll of the late Eastern Han Dynasty and the Three Kingdoms, and mainly describes the political conflicts and military struggles among the Three Kingdoms: Wei, Shu and Wu. Besides creating a large number of heroes in a chaotic world such as Liu Bei, Zhuge Liang, Cao Cao and Sun Quan, the book also artistically relives many battles like the Battle of Guandu and the Battle of Chibi.

This novel had a great impact on later literary works. Since its publication, numerous historical romance novels have emerged in succession and various dramas on "the Three Kingdoms" have been created one after another. Even today, characters in the Three Kingdoms are favored materials for online games as well as comics and animations.

The Grace of Kings

The Grace of Kings is a fantasy novel, in which a mysterious nation consisting of many islands is described. Like *Romance of the Three Kingdoms*, this novel also creates some heroes and tells numerous legends. It is said that the author drew inspiration from the Chu-Han War.

The Grace of Kings, which combines Chinese history with Western culture, was written by Ken Liu, a Chinese American author of science fiction. This book won the Locus Award in 2016.

Discussion

1. Of Liu Bei, Guan Yu and Zhang Fei, which character do you like best? Why?
2. Is literature, especially historical fiction, good or bad for people to learn about history? Why?

拾伍　桃园结义

引

广为流传的词作《临江仙·滚滚长江东逝水》是明代杨慎所作，后被罗贯中引用，成为《三国演义》的开篇之词。这是一曲感慨宇宙永恒、英雄人物转瞬即逝的咏叹调。整首词如下：

滚滚长江东逝水，浪花淘尽英雄。是非成败转头空。青山依旧在，几度夕阳红。

白发渔樵江渚上，惯看秋月春风。一壶浊酒喜相逢。古今多少事，都付笑谈中。

以下故事改编自《三国演义》。

◎《三国演义》插图
描绘刘、关、张桃园结义

故事

东汉末年，战火纷飞。朝廷发榜，招募士兵，这立即引起了一位英雄的注意。这位英雄便是刘备，当时正以卖草鞋为生。

见到皇榜，刘备长叹一声。忽然，他听到身后有一个声音，响如惊雷。“你为何长叹，而不去为国家出力？”

刘备转过身来，立刻意识到此人绝非碌碌之辈。这个人是张飞，刘备向他介绍自己道：“我叫刘备，一直梦想平定天下，但无能为力。”

“我有一点资产。共同干一番大事如何？”张飞道。刘备十分高兴，于是两人去了一个小酒馆谈论他们的大计。

正当他们饮酒之时，进来一人。此人身材魁梧，留着长长的胡须，脸色深红，让人望而生畏。这便是关羽，他很快与刘张二人一起谈论起来。三人聊了很久，发现他们志趣相投。最终，他们决定结拜为兄弟。

第二日，他们去了张飞的农场。此时，桃花盛开，香烟袅袅。三人发誓道：“刘备、关羽、张飞，虽为异姓，然在此结为兄弟，今后定当同心协力，保国安民。不求同年同月同日生，只愿同年同月同日死。”

三人当中，刘备为兄长，关羽居中，张飞为弟。

《桃园结义》
北京中山公园长廊画作

文化链接

《三国演义》

《三国演义》是中国“古典长篇小说四大名著”之一，作者是元末明初的罗贯中。

《三国演义》展现了一幅东汉末年和三国时代的历史画卷，主要描写了魏、蜀、吴三国之间的政治纷争和军事斗争。该书塑造了一大批乱世英雄，比如刘备、诸葛亮、曹操、孙权。除此以外，还艺术地再现了很多战役，比如官渡之战、赤壁之战。

这部小说对后世的文学作品影响极大。自该书问世后，很多历史演义小说相继出现，各类关于“三国”的戏剧层出不穷。甚至在今天，三国人物也是网游和动漫的热门题材。

《蒲公英王朝》

《蒲公英王朝》是一部奇幻小说，描述了一个由众多岛屿构成的神秘国度。同《三国演义》一样，这部小说也塑造了一些英雄人物，讲述了很多传奇故事。据说作者从楚汉战争中汲取了灵感。

《蒲公英王朝》是中国历史与西方文化的融合，作者是刘宇昆，美国华裔科幻小说家。2016年，该书获轨迹奖。

讨论

1. 在刘备、关羽、张飞之中，你最喜欢哪个人物？为什么？
2. 文学，尤其是历史小说，对人们了解历史有益还是有害？为什么？

XVI YU BOYA BREAKING HIS ZITHER IN HONOR OF A FAITHFUL FRIEND

Introduction

Bo Ya, a famous zither player during the Spring and Autumn Period, was born in the Chu State and later served as an official in the Jin State. He has been renowned for his friendship with Zhong Ziqi and for the melody *High Mountains and Flowing Water*. This melody is one of the "Top 10 Chinese Classical Melodies" and is said to be composed by Bo Ya. The name of this melody later became a Chinese idiom, which is often used to indicate a faithful friend is hard to find. The Chinese expression *zhiyin* (which literally means "to know the tone") originates from the story about Bo Ya and Zhong Ziqi, and it is used to describe a close and sympathetic friend.

The story about Bo Ya and Zhong Ziqi is widespread among people and it was first recorded in the book *Liezi*. It was compiled into *Stories to Caution the World* by Feng Menglong, a man of letters in the Ming Dynasty. In this book, Bo Ya was named "Yu Boya" by the author.

The following story is adapted from *Stories to Caution the World*.

⊙ The Ancient Zither Platform (also called "Yu Boya Platform"), said to be where Bo Ya met his faithful friend Zhong Ziqi, located at the foot of Mount Tortoise in Wuhan City of Hubei Province

Story Time

Yu Boya was a master zither player, but he felt lonely since no one could understand his music. One autumn, Yu Boya and his entourage sailed along the Yangtze River to pay an official visit to the Chu State.

On the night of the Mid-Autumn Festival, they arrived at the mouth of the Hanjiang River. Suddenly, a storm raged and they had to moor the boat at the foot of a hill. After the storm stopped, Yu Boya started to play the zither in the clear moonlight.

At this moment, a woodcutter named Zhong Ziqi, who stood under a rock to shelter from the rain, was enjoying himself in the beautiful music. Knowing that Zhong Ziqi had listened for quite a while, Yu Boya invited him to board the boat and continued to play a new melody.

After the first part, Zhong Ziqi exclaimed in delight, "What a moving part! It is as magnificent as Mount Tai!" Yu Boya then played another part and Zhong Ziqi blurted, "What a touching part! It is as powerful as the rivers!" Whatever Yu Boya wanted to express in his music, Zhong Ziqi never failed to understand. They chatted for a long time and took turns proposing toasts.

As the first glimmer of dawn lit the sky, Yu Boya rose and said, "How amazing … My good brother, I met you too late!" They made an appointment to meet at the following Mid-Autumn Festival.

The next year, Yu Boya returned to the place on time and waited for the whole night, only to find Zhong Ziqi had died of a sudden disease months before. He came to Zhong Ziqi's tomb and sadly played *High Mountains and Flowing Water*. After he finished, he broke the strings and smashed the zither to commemorate his faithful friend, the only one who could understand this melody. He vowed never to play it anymore.

⊙ The scenery around the stone carving *High Mountains and Flowing Water* in Mount Tai, said to interpret the charm of the melody

Cultural Links

Three Words and Two Hits

Stories to Caution the World is a vernacular story collection compiled by Feng Menglong, preceded by *Stories to Enlighten the World* and followed by *Stories to Awaken the World*. Since the title of each story collection ends with the Chinese character 言, the three story collections are collectively known as 三言 (Three Words). Each one contains 40 stories, which provide a vivid description of Chinese social life before the end of the Ming Dynasty.

It is said that the success of the "Three Words" inspired Ling Mengchu to complete two story collections, namely *Slapping the Table in Amazement I* and *Slapping the Table in Amazement II*, which are collectively called 二拍 (Two Hits).

"Three Words and Two Hits" is the pinnacle of classical short stories in the vernacular.

Traditional Chinese musical instruments

The images of traditional musical instruments appear frequently in classical literature, such as Liu Changqing's "The seven-stringed zither tinkles; I hear the soughs through the pines", Li Shangyin's "I wonder why the zither has 50 strings; each pluck, each stop, recalls the vanished springs", and Lu You's "Pipes and drums are to boom in the spring sacrifice near; villagers dressed simply are to honor old ways here".

In ancient China, musical instruments were divided into eight categories, which were called *bayin*. They were respectively made of eight kinds of materials: silk, bamboo, wood, stone, metal, clay, gourd and skin.

Zithers are silk instruments. According to the number of strings, zithers can be categorized into *guqin* (usually seven strings), *se* (usually 25 strings), *guzheng* (usually 21 strings), etc. In the above story, what Yu Boya played is *guqin*. Some other traditional musical instruments, such as the bowed string instrument *erhu* (two-stringed fiddle), the plucked string instrument *pipa* (usually four strings) and the struck string instrument *yangqin* (hit by two hammers), are often used to play traditional Chinese music.

Apart from the instruments mentioned above, there are other traditional Chinese musical instruments like the bamboo instruments *dizi* and *xiao*, the wood instrument *bangzi*, and the metal instruments *bianzhong* (bronze bells hung on a wooden frame and struck with a mallet), *suona* (a trumpet-shaped brass instrument), and *luo* (a flat, circular metal disc).

◎ Playing the *pipa*

◎ Playing the *sanxian*

◎ Playing the *dizi*

◎ Playing the *xiao*

◎ Playing the *luo*

The story of Goethe and Schiller

In Weimar, Germany stands a statue of two German literary giants (Goethe and Schiller) standing side by side. Goethe, born in 1749, and Schiller, 10 years younger than him, maintained a friendship for over 10 years.

Goethe and Schiller discussed each other's works, as well as those of their contemporaries, and jointly composed a collection of satirical epigrams, *Xenien*. Their remarks and writings were very influential in the literary circle, promoting the development of German literature.

⊙ The Goethe-Schiller Monument, located in Weimar, Germany

Discussion

1. If you were Yu Boya, would you break the zither after Zhong Ziqi died? Why?
2. According to the story of Yu Boya and Zhong Ziqi and that of Goethe and Schiller, can you describe what friendship is? Please share your ideas.

拾陆　俞伯牙摔琴谢知音

引

伯牙是春秋时期著名的琴师，生于楚国，后在晋国做官，因与钟子期的友情及乐曲《高山流水》而闻名。此曲为“中国十大古典名曲”之一，相传为伯牙所作。曲名后来也成为一则成语，常用来指知音难觅。汉语词汇“知音”（字面意思是“懂得音律”）源自伯牙和钟子期的故事，用来形容亲密相通的朋友。

伯牙和钟子期的故事在民间广为流传，最早记载于《列子》一书中。明代的文学家冯梦龙将其编入《警世通言》。在这本书中，作者将伯牙称作“俞伯牙”。

以下故事就是根据《警世通言》改编而来的。

◎ 古琴台（亦称“俞伯牙台”）
相传伯牙在此处遇到他的知音钟子期
位于湖北省武汉市龟山脚下

故事

俞伯牙是抚琴高手，但无人能听懂他的琴声，因而他感到寂寞。有一年秋天，俞伯牙和随从沿长江乘船出使楚国。

正值中秋之夜，他们来到了汉江江口。突然风雨大作，他们不得不将船停在一座小山下。风雨平息之后，月光朗朗，俞伯牙便开始抚琴。

此刻，在岩石下避雨的樵夫钟子期，正沉醉在这优美的琴声之中。得知钟子期已听了好一会儿，俞伯牙就邀请他上船，自己则继续弹奏新曲。

第一段奏毕，钟子期开心地叹道："这部分多么动人啊！它如泰山一般雄伟！"然后俞伯牙又弹奏了一段，钟子期脱口而出："这部分多么感人啊！它如江河一般激荡！"无论俞伯牙想要在琴声中表达什么，钟子期都能明白。他们聊了很久，轮番敬酒。

当曙光点亮天空时，俞伯牙起身说道："太妙了……好兄弟，真是相见恨晚啊！"他们约定来年的中秋再相会。

第二年，俞伯牙如期回到了那个地方。他等了整整一晚，却发现钟子期已于数月前突然染病去世。俞伯牙来到钟子期的坟前，悲伤地奏起了《高山流水》。奏罢，他断弦摔琴，以纪念唯一听懂此曲的知音，并发誓不再演奏这首乐曲。

◎ 泰山《高山流水》石刻周边风景
据说此地风景诠释了该曲的神韵

文化链接

三言二拍

《警世通言》是冯梦龙编撰的白话小说集，完成于《醒世恒言》之前，《喻世明言》之后。每本小说集均以汉字“言”结尾，因而这三本小说集合称“三言”（Three Words）。每本小说集都有四十个故事，这些故事生动地呈现了明末之前中国的社会生活。

据说“三言”的成功让凌濛初得到了启发，完成了两本小说集，即《初刻拍案惊奇》和《二刻拍案惊奇》。这两本小说集合称“二拍”（Two Hits）。

“三言二拍”是古典短篇白话小说的巅峰之作。

中国传统乐器

传统乐器的意象常常出现在古典文学中，比如刘长卿的“泠泠七弦上，静听松风寒”，李商隐的“锦瑟无端五十弦，一弦一柱思华年”，陆游的“箫鼓追随春社近，衣冠简朴古风存”。

在古代中国，乐器被分成八类，称为“八音”。它们分别由八种材料制成：丝、竹、木、石、金、土、匏、革。

琴属于丝乐器。根据弦的数量，琴可以分为古琴（通常为七弦）、瑟（通常为二十五弦）、古筝（通常为二十一弦）等。在上述故事中，俞伯牙弹的是古琴。一些其他传统乐器，比如弓弦乐器二胡（两弦提琴）、拨弦乐器琵琶（通常为四弦）、击弦乐器扬琴（用两个琴竹击打），也常用来演奏中国传统音乐。

除了上面提到的乐器之外，还有一些其他的中国传统乐器，如：竹乐器笛子和箫，木乐器梆子，金属乐器编钟（悬挂在木架上、用木槌击打的铜钟）、唢呐（铜制喇叭状乐器）、锣（扁平的圆形金属盘）。

◎ 弹琵琶

◎ 弹三弦

◎ 吹笛子

◎ 吹箫

◎ 敲锣

歌德和席勒的故事

在德国魏玛，矗立着一座两位德国文学巨匠（歌德和席勒）并肩而立的雕像。歌德出生于1749年，席勒比他小了十岁，他们之间保持了十余年的友谊。

歌德和席勒讨论彼此的作品以及同时代作家的作品，并共同创作了讽刺诗集《克赛尼恩》。他们的言论和著作在文学界很有影响力，推动了德国文学的发展。

◎ 歌德席勒纪念碑位于德国魏玛

讨论

1. 如果你是俞伯牙，钟子期过世之后你会摔琴吗？为什么？
2. 根据俞伯牙和钟子期以及歌德和席勒的故事，你能描述一下什么是友谊吗？请分享你的想法。

XVII THE TAOIST PRIEST OF LAOSHAN

Introduction

"The Taoist Priest of Laoshan" is a famous story from *Strange Stories from a Chinese Studio* and depicts a flighty and impetuous young man who cannot endure hardships when learning the Taoist mysteries and finally becomes a failure. The author used this story to satirize those who wish to succeed without any effort.

Strange Stories from a Chinese Studio was written by Pu Songling, who is regarded as one of the most celebrated men of letters of the Qing Dynasty. The following story is adapted from *Strange Stories from a Chinese Studio*.

⊙ Pu Songling's study, located in the former residence of Pu Songling in Zibo City of Shandong Province

Story Time

There lived in our town a scholar surnamed Wang, who had been admiring Taoist mysteries. Hearing that there were crowds of immortals on Mount Laoshan, Wang packed his bag and went to find them. At the peak, he found a priest apparently with profound mysteries. After Wang expressed his determination to learn Taoist mysteries, he was allowed by the priest to stay in the temple.

Early the next morning, the priest summoned Wang, asking him to chop wood with other disciples. Wang obeyed the priest's command and continued the same work for the following two months. With calluses on hands and feet, he could not stand it any longer, thinking about returning home.

Wang finally said farewell to the priest. He said, "Master, I've been here for two months. I chop wood every day, learning nothing at all. I once saw you walk through the wall. Could you teach me this skill to make my stay here worthwhile?" The priest agreed and taught the incantation to him. Then, the priest said loudly, "Now, run through the wall. Put your head down and rush toward it!" Wang took a few steps back, ran toward the wall at full speed, and surprisingly found himself on the other side of the wall. The priest told him to use this skill with caution, otherwise it would not work. Delighted, Wang thanked the priest and then left.

After he got home, Wang bragged to his wife about the skill of walking through the wall. His wife totally disbelieved him, so he decided to demonstrate this skill. He moved backward, put his head down, and dashed into the wall. With a loud bang, he fell in a heap on the floor.

⊙ Mount Laoshan, said to be a sacred site of Taoism, situated in Qingdao City of Shandong Province

Cultural Links

Classical fiction in the Qing Dynasty

Classical fiction of China reached an all-time peak in the Ming and Qing dynasties, when a large number of excellent novels and short stories appeared. These works of fiction are characterized by compact plots and varied themes (romance, heroism, ghosts, foxes, immortals, demons, etc).

The most celebrated works of fiction in the Qing Dynasty are *Strange Stories from a Chinese Studio* by Pu Songling, *Unofficial History of the Scholars* by Wu Jingzi, etc.

Strange Stories from a Chinese Studio

Strange Stories from a Chinese Studio, written by Pu Songling, is a collection of supernatural short stories. The main characters of this book are not ordinary people, but ghosts, foxes, immortals and demons. The author used this book to deplore the decadent feudal system and express his desire for an ideal world.

The Metamorphosis

The Metamorphosis, one of the most popular novellas written by Franz Kafka, was first published in 1915. The main character of the story is Gregor Samsa, who worked as a salesman. As Gregor woke up from a nightmare one morning, he found himself transformed into a gigantic insect. To his greater disappointment, his family also changed their attitude toward him. They forced him to stay in the bedroom, threw apples at him, and kept away from him. Eventually, Gregor died in loneliness and despair.

Discussion

1. Why did the scholar in the story fail to walk through the wall at home?

2. "The Taoist Priest of Laoshan" and *The Metamorphosis* are both supernatural satires. Which one do you prefer? Why?

拾柒　崂山道士

引

《崂山道士》是《聊斋志异》中一个著名的故事，描绘了一个心浮气躁的年轻人。他修习道术时吃不了苦，以失败告终。作者用这个故事讽刺了那些不付出努力就想获得成功的人。

《聊斋志异》的作者是蒲松龄，他被认为是清代最著名的文学家之一。以下故事就是根据《聊斋志异》改编而来的。

◎ 蒲松龄书房，位于山东省淄博市的蒲松龄故居

故事

我们县里有个王姓书生，向来仰慕道术。他听说崂山上仙人成群，就收拾好包袱，前去寻找仙人。在山顶，他找到了一位看似道术高深的道士。在王生表明了自己习道的决心之后，道士就同意让他留在观中。

第二天一早，道士把王生叫来，让他随其他门徒去砍柴。王生听从了道士的命令。此后两月，王生每天都做着同样的事。他手脚生茧，无法再忍受，考虑着回家。

王生终于向道士辞行了。他说："师父，我来此已有两月，每日砍柴，什么都没学到。我曾看到您穿墙而过。您能否将此技艺传授于我，好让弟子不虚此行？"道士答应了，将咒语教给了他。然后，道士大声说道："现在，跑着穿过墙。低下头，朝它冲过去！"王生退后几步，全速向墙跑去，惊讶地发现自己到了墙的另一边。道士叮嘱他慎用此技，否则技艺会失效。王生很高兴，谢过道士后就离开了。

回到家后，王生向妻子炫耀穿墙术。他的妻子完全不相信他，因此他决定展示一下这项技艺。他往后退了下，低下头，向墙冲去。砰的一声，王生倒在了地上，一动不动了。

◎ 崂山
据说是道教圣地
位于山东省青岛市

文化链接

清代古典小说

明清时期是中国古典小说的巅峰时期，涌现出大量优秀的长篇小说与短篇小说。这些小说作品的特点是情节紧凑，话题（爱情、侠义、鬼狐仙怪等）多样。

清代最著名的小说作品有蒲松龄的《聊斋志异》、吴敬梓的《儒林外史》等。

《聊斋志异》

《聊斋志异》是一部短篇灵异故事合集，作者是蒲松龄。该书的主要人物不是凡人，而是鬼狐仙怪。作者借此书抨击了腐朽的封建制度，表达了他对理想世界的向往。

《变形记》

《变形记》是弗朗茨·卡夫卡最受欢迎的中篇小说之一，最早出版于1915年。故事的主人公是格雷戈尔·萨姆萨，他是一名销售员。有一天早上，当格雷戈尔从噩梦中醒来时，发现自己变成了一条巨虫。更令他沮丧的是，他的家人对他的态度也转变了。他们强迫他呆在卧室，朝他扔苹果，远离他。最终，格雷戈尔在孤独与绝望中死去。

讨论

1. 故事中的书生在家穿墙时为什么会失败?
2.《崂山道士》和《变形记》都属于灵异类讽刺作品。你更喜欢哪一个？为什么?

XVIII FAN JIN SUCCEEDING IN THE IMPERIAL EXAMINATION AT THE PROVINCIAL LEVEL

Introduction

Fan Jin is a famous character in the novel *Unofficial History of the Scholars*. Since his 20s, he had determined to pass the imperial examination. Unfortunately, he failed numerous times and had to live in poverty with his old mother and his wife for decades, for which he was despised and even abused by his father-in-law, Butcher Hu. Fan Jin could do nothing but endure it silently. Unexpectedly, one day in his 50s, he succeeded in the imperial examination at the provincial level.

The following story is adapted from *Unofficial History of the Scholars*. A pedantic scholar, who is in keen pursuit of official rank, is shown forth in Wu Jingzi's writing.

⊙ A statue of Wu Jingzi, housed in the Museum of Anhui Notables in Hefei City of Anhui Province

Story Time

Fan Jin was selling chicken at the fair when the news came that he had succeeded in the imperial examination at the provincial level. After coming back home, Fan Jin spotted the messengers and the official notice. He could hardly believe what he saw, so he took another look, with his eyes opened wide. He then clapped and laughed, saying "Terrific! I got it!" Immediately he fell onto the ground, unconscious.

Seeing this, his mother was so scared that she immediately gave her son some water to drink. Fan Jin soon woke up and then ran out, clapping and shouting, "Terrific! I got it!"

Hardly had Fan Jin covered a few steps when he fell into a bog, his hair messy and his hands muddy. He struggled to crawl out and shouted all the way to the fair like a lunatic, leaving his mother and his wife at a loss.

"Lord Fan just lost his mind out of ecstasy. Whom is he scared of most? If this person slaps him on the face, Lord Fan will recover," proposed one man.

"His father-in-law, Butcher Hu, of course!" answered another man.

Informed of this, Butcher Hu felt quite upset. "How dare I? My son-in-law as Fan Jin is, he is a lord now," he said.

After people tried every possible way to persuade him, Butcher Hu finally agreed. He drank two bowls of liquor and plucked up his courage to come to the fair. Fan Jin was standing by the gate of a temple, clapping and shouting, "I got it! I got it!" Butcher Hu walked toward him and hit him in the face, saying "You damn fool! What the hell have you got?" Fan Jin was knocked out. After a short while, he woke up and regained his sanity.

⊙ A set of stamps depicting six stories (first row, second from left: Fan Jin Succeeding in the Imperial Examination at the Provincial Level) in *Unofficial History of the Scholars*, issued by China Post

Cultural Links

Unofficial History of the Scholars

Unofficial History of the Scholars, a novel written by Wu Jingzi of the Qing Dynasty, is a biting satire on the social system at that time. It is regarded as a masterpiece of ancient Chinese satirical novels. Lu Xun believes that this book is "impartial and objective in criticizing social issues of the time" while Hu Shi holds that this book is featured by "sketchy and silhouetted figures".

Unofficial History of the Scholars had a great impact on the history of Chinese novels. Since its publication, a large number of condemnation novels, such as *A Flower in a Sinful Sea, Bizarre Happenings Eyewitnessed over Two Decades* and *Officialdom Unmasked*, have come out, setting a trend of criticizing the society.

Yan Jiansheng

Besides Fan Jin, Wu Jingzi also created numerous classic characters in *Unofficial History of the Scholars*. Yan Jiansheng is one of them.

Yan Jiansheng was a typical miser—he refused to close his eyes at the point of death because he saw two wicks burning at the same time. This image strikes root in the hearts of people and it is comparable to the four great misers in world literature (Shakespeare's Shylock, Balzac's Grandet, Molière's Harpagon, and Gogol's Plyushkin).

The Chameleon

"The Chameleon" is a short story written by Chekhov, a literary giant of Russia. The main character of this story, Otchumyelov, was compared to a chameleon (a small lizard that can change color according to its surroundings), and his attitude toward a dog changed six times within just a few minutes. With superb skill in satire, Chekhov exposed the ugliness of the feudal society under the cover of grandeur.

The word "chameleon" has become a symbol, and it is frequently used to satirize those who bend with the winds.

Discussion

1. Why did Fan Jin behave so unusually after succeeding in the imperial examination at the provincial level?
2. What are the similarities between Butcher Hu and Otchumyelov?

拾捌　范进中举

引

范进是小说《儒林外史》中一个著名的人物。他自二十几岁就下定决心要通过科举考试。不幸的是，几十年来，他屡屡失败，不得不与老母和妻子过着穷困潦倒的生活。岳父胡屠户也因此看不起他，甚至辱骂他。范进什么也做不了，只能默默忍受。意想不到的是，在五十几岁的某一天，他中了举人。

以下故事改编自《儒林外史》。在吴敬梓的笔下，一个迂腐而热衷功名的读书人跃然纸上。

◎ 吴敬梓雕像
藏于安徽省合肥市的安徽名人馆

故事

范进中举的消息传来时，他正在集市上卖鸡。回到家后，范进一眼就认出了报信人和报帖。他难以相信眼前所见，故而睁大眼睛又看了一遍，然后拍手大笑道："太好了！我中了！"紧接着他就倒在了地上，不省人事。

见此情景，范老太太害怕了，连忙给她儿子喂了几口水。范进很快醒了过来，然后跑了出去，边拍手边喊道："太好了！我中了！"

刚走了没几步，范进就掉进了泥塘里，头发散乱，两手黄泥。他挣扎着爬出来，一路叫着去了集市，像个疯子一样，令他的母亲和娘子不知如何是好。

一个人出主意道："范老爷只因太高兴而迷了心窍。他最怕谁？只要这个人打他一耳光，他就会恢复过来。"

"当然是他的岳父胡屠户！"另一人回答。

得知此事，胡屠户觉得很不安。他说："我怎么敢呢？虽然范进是我女婿，如今他却成了老爷。"

人们好说歹说，胡屠户终于同意了。他喝了两碗酒，鼓起勇气来到集市。范进正站在一座庙的门口，边拍手边喊道："我中了！我中了！"胡屠户朝他走过去，打了他一耳光，说道："你这个该死的笨蛋！你究竟中了什么？"范进被打昏了。不一会儿，他醒了过来，恢复了神智。

◎ 一套描绘《儒林外史》中六个故事（第一行左二：《范进中举》）的邮票由中国邮政发行

文化链接

《儒林外史》

《儒林外史》是清代吴敬梓创作的一部小说，是对当时社会体系的辛辣讽刺。它被认为是中国古代讽刺小说的杰作。鲁迅认为该书“秉持公心，指擿时弊”，胡适认为该书的一个特色是“速写式和剪影式的人物形象”。

《儒林外史》对中国小说史产生了很大的影响。自该书问世后，一大批谴责小说出现，如《孽海花》、《二十年目睹之怪现状》、《官场现形记》，形成了一股批判社会的潮流。

严监生

除了范进，吴敬梓还在《儒林外史》中塑造了许多经典人物，严监生就是其中之一。

严监生是典型的吝啬鬼——他临死前因为看到两根灯芯同时燃烧着就不肯闭眼。这个形象深入人心，可以和世界文学作品中的四大吝啬鬼（莎士比亚笔下的夏洛克、巴尔扎克笔下的葛朗台、莫里哀笔下的阿巴贡、果戈里笔下的普柳什金）相提并论。

《变色龙》

《变色龙》是俄国文学巨匠契诃夫所写的一篇短篇小说。这个故事的主人公奥楚蔑洛夫被比作“变色龙”（一种可以根据环境变色的小蜥蜴）。在仅仅几分钟内，他对一只狗的态度就转变了六次。契诃夫运用卓越的讽刺技巧，揭露了在华丽外表掩盖下的封建社会的丑恶。

“变色龙”这个词已经成为一个符号，常用来讽刺那些见风使舵的人。

讨论

1. 范进中举后为什么会有如此异常的表现?

2. 胡屠户和奥楚蔑洛夫有什么相似之处?

XIX THE FIRST MEETING OF BAOYU AND DAIYU

Introduction

Classical gardens of China are landscape gardens represented by royal gardens in the north and private gardens in the south, and they are in pursuit of harmony the between humanity and nature. Classical gardens of China are important legacies of human civilization.

The Grand View Garden, an important complex in the novel *Dream of the Red Chamber*, is a magnificent, beautiful classical garden. It incorporates the best part of the southern and northern gardens in its planning and layout. In the novel, it is the place where Jia Baoyu and his family lived.

The following story is adapted from *Dream of the Red Chamber*, describing the scene when Lin Daiyu stepped into the Jia Manor for the first time and met Jia Baoyu.

Part of the Grand View Garden, painted by Sun Wen of the Qing Dynasty

Story Time

Shortly after Daiyu entered the Jia Manor, a waiting maid announced,"Baoyu is coming!" Daiyu was thinking about what this good-for-nothing boy would be like when a young man walked in. His face was like the full moon at Mid-Autumn; his complexion was like the morning flowers in spring. Daiyu was taken aback and thought, "How strange! He looks so familiar! It's as if I have seen him somewhere before."

After changing his clothes, Baoyu came back to greet Daiyu. "This cousin is different from any other girls," he thought. "In her quietness, she is much like a beautiful flower reflected in the water and when she walks, she is as tender as a willow twig against the breeze." Baoyu said with a smile, "I have seen this cousin before." "What nonsense! How could you have seen her before?" remarked Dowager Lady Jia. Baoyu replied, "I may not have seen her before, but she looks so familiar as if we were old acquaintances. It feels as if we reunited today after a long separation."

Baoyu then sat beside Daiyu and asked, "Have you got jade?" People around were confused about the question and so was Daiyu. She replied, "No, I haven't. How could everyone have it as it is so rare?" Hearing this, Baoyu burst out crying, throwing his jade on the floor. "It is rare!" With tears streaming down his face, he shouted, "It can't even distinguish who is noble from average people. None of my cousins have it. Here comes this beautiful cousin. She doesn't have it either! So, why do I need it?"

It took a long while for Dowager Lady Jia to persuade Baoyu to wear the jade again.

⊙ Lin Daiyu Being at the Bamboo Lodge of the Jia Manor, painted by Yan Shaoxiang

Cultural Links

Dream of the Red Chamber

Dream of the Red Chamber, also called *The Story of the Stone*, is one of China's "Four Great Classical Novels". In the novel, the author described the rise and fall of four aristocratic clans—the clan of Jia, Wang, Shi and Xue—and presented to readers various aspects of Chinese culture, including poetry, medicine, cuisine, tea, Confucianism, Buddhism, Taoism, filial piety, opera, music and architecture.

Redology

Redology is a subject that studies the novel *Dream of the Red Chamber* and its related issues, and according to the findings and characteristics of the research, it can be divided into two stages: old redology and new redology. Old redology refers to research work done from the Qing Dynasty to the early years of the Republic of China, and it mainly employs methods of commentary, index, etc. After the May Fourth Movement, Hu Shi, Yu Pingbo and others created new redology in the process of criticizing old redology, and expanded the research fields of redology.

Remarks on *Dream of the Red Chamber*

In terms of only the theme of the story, it varies from reader to reader. A Confucianism scholar sees *Book of Changes*, a moralist sees pornography, a gifted young scholar sees sentiment, a revolutionist sees anti-Qing thoughts and a gossip sees court affairs.

—Lu Xun

Dream of the Red Chamber is a book of philosophy, of the universe as well as of literature. The value of this book lies in that it goes against our traditional national spirit ... Instead of a comedy, the book *Dream of the Red Chamber* is an out-and-out tragedy.

—Wang Guowei

If you want to understand the cultural characteristics of China, the best way—the most interesting and convenient (as well as concrete, distinct and lively) way—is to read through *Dream of the Red Chamber*.

—Zhou Ruchang

Of all the classic Chinese novels, *The Story of the Stone* ... is indisputably the greatest masterpiece.

—Frederic Wakeman Jr.

The Tale of Genji

The Tale of Genji is a classic work of Japanese literature, and it was written by Murasaki Shikibu, a female writer of Japan. The book mainly tells the stories of the hero Hikaru Genji and the many women around him, and depicts the life of the aristocracy at that time.

The Tale of Genji bears a striking resemblance to *Dream of the Red Chamber* in many aspects. In both works, many well-developed major and minor characters are created, a large number of poems are adopted, and the rise and fall of an era is reflected through love stories. Most strikingly, both works include some beautiful and talented females. Their miserable fates embody the authors' strong indictment against the feudal society.

Discussion

1. Some people say Baoyu falls in love with Daiyu at the first sight. Do you believe in love at the first sight? Why?
2. Both *The Tale of Genji* and *Dream of the Red Chamber* tell tragic stories. What other tragic works do you know? Why do they move you deeply?

拾玖　宝黛初见

引

中国古典园林是以北方皇家园林和南方私家园林为代表的山水园林，追求人与自然的和谐。中国古典园林是人类文明的重要遗产。

小说《红楼梦》中的重要建筑大观园就是一座宏伟、秀丽的古典园林，在规划布局方面吸收了南北园林的精华。在小说中，大观园是贾宝玉和他的家人居住的地方。

以下故事改编自《红楼梦》，描写的是林黛玉初进贾府时遇到贾宝玉的场景。

◎ 大观园局部
清代孙温绘

故事

黛玉进贾府不久，丫环就说道：“宝玉来了！”黛玉正想着这个惫懒的公子是什么样子的，这时一个年轻男子走了进来。他面如中秋之月，色如春晓之花。黛玉大吃一惊，心里想：“好生奇怪，他看上去如此眼熟，我似乎在哪里见过他。”

换了衣服后，宝玉回来问候黛玉。“这位妹妹与其他姑娘有所不同。”他心想。“她娴静时如姣花照水，行动处似弱柳扶风。”宝玉笑道：“这个妹妹我曾见过。”贾母道：“胡说！你何曾见过她？”宝玉答道：“或许我未曾见过她，但她看上去如此眼熟，仿佛我们是旧相识。今日，感觉我们倒像是久别重逢。”

然后，宝玉在黛玉身边坐下，问道：“你有玉吗？”周围的人对这个问题感到不解，黛玉也一样。她答道：“没有，我没有。那块玉如此稀罕，岂能人人都有？”听了这话，宝玉顿时大哭起来，把他的玉扔在了地上。“算什么稀罕物！”他泪流满面，大声说道：“它连人的高低都不分。家里姐姐妹妹都没有。如今来了一个漂亮的妹妹，她也没有。那么我为什么要它？”

贾母花了好久才说服宝玉将玉重新戴上。

◎ 林黛玉在贾府潇湘馆
晏少翔绘

文化链接

《红楼梦》

《红楼梦》，又称《石头记》，是中国“古典长篇小说四大名著”之一。在这部小说中，作者描绘了贾、王、史、薛四大家族的兴衰，向读者介绍了中国文化的方方面面，包括诗歌、医药、烹饪、茶、儒、释、道、孝、戏剧、音乐、建筑。

红学

红学是研究小说《红楼梦》及相关课题的学科。按研究成果与研究特点，红学可分为两个阶段：旧红学和新红学。旧红学指清代至民国初年的研究，以评注法、索引法等研究方法为主。五四运动后，胡适、俞平伯等人在批判旧红学的过程中建立了新红学，扩大了红学的研究领域。

关于《红楼梦》的评语

单是命意，就因读者的眼光而有种种，经学家看见《易》，道学家看见淫，才子看见缠绵，革命家看见排满，流言家看见宫闱秘事。

——鲁迅

《红楼梦》，哲学的也，宇宙的也，文学的也。此《红楼梦》之所以大背于吾国人之精神，而其价值亦即存乎此……《红楼梦》一书，与一切喜剧相反，彻头彻尾之悲剧也。

——王国维

如果你想要了解中华民族的文化特点特色，最好的——既最有趣味又最为捷便（具体、真切、生动）的办法就是去读通了《红楼梦》。

——周汝昌

在所有的中国古典小说中，《石头记》……毫无疑问是最伟大的杰作。

——小弗雷德里克·韦克曼

《源氏物语》

《源氏物语》是日本文学的经典之作，由日本女作家紫式部创作。该书主要讲述了主人公光源氏与他身边众多女性的故事，描绘了当时的贵族阶层的生活。

《源氏物语》与《红楼梦》在许多方面有着惊人的相似之处。两部作品都塑造了大量形象丰满的主要角色和次要角色，都采用了大量诗歌，都通过爱情故事反映了时代的兴衰。最突出的是，两部作品中都有一些美丽又有才华的女性。她们的悲惨命运体现了作者对封建社会的强烈控诉。

讨论

1. 有人说宝玉对黛玉一见钟情。你相信一见钟情吗？为什么？
2.《源氏物语》与《红楼梦》讲述的都是悲剧故事。你还知道哪些悲剧作品？它们为什么能深深地打动你？

XX LIAN JINFENG

Introduction

In 1924, the Peking opera *Lian Jinfeng* starring Mei Lanfang was performed in Japan. It achieved smashing success, which contributed to the shooting of a Peking opera film consisting of two acts from Mei Lanfang's two representative works. The film was later screened in various regions in Japan and won popularity with the Japanese audience.

Like the Peking opera and the film mentioned above, the following story is also adapted from the novel *Flowers in the Mirror*.

⊙ Lian Jinfeng in the Peking opera, acted by Ge Xiangru

Story Time

Lian Jinfeng was a dutiful daughter living in the Land of the Virtuous. After her father died in exile, she alone took care of her mother, who was in poor health. Knowing that sea cucumbers could treat her mother's disease, she trained hard in diving and captured sea cucumbers from the sea regularly. Since then, her mother had gradually got better.

One day, to capture sea cucumbers, she carried her sword and dived into the deep sea as usual. But this time, she was caught in a net, with which a fisherman and his wife were fishing. Seeing the girl, beautiful and young, the couple immediately tied her up and planned to sell her at a good price. At that time, a big ship was approaching. Lian Jinfeng cried for help.

A scholar named Tang Ao was traveling around various countries with his friends and was just passing by. Hearing someone crying for help, Tang Ao and his friends sped toward the shore.

Lian Jinfeng told them, "My great grandparents originally lived in Lingnan. To flee from the chaos of the war, they moved to the Land of the Virtuous. I have read numerous poetical works since childhood. Today, I came to this place to capture sea cucumbers for my mother but was accidentally caught by the fisherman. They are going to sell me. Please help me!" To prove her case, Lian Jinfeng wrote down a seven-character-a-line quatrain to describe her experiences.

Tang Ao recognized her as a woman of both ability and integrity. Immediately, he took out 100 taels of silver to exchange for Lian Jinfeng's freedom.

To repay Tang Ao for saving her, Lian Jinfeng jumped into the sea again and fought against the mussel, obtaining a big pearl which she presented to him.

⊙ A stage photo of Lian Jinfeng piercing the mussel, taken from the Peking opera *Lian Jinfeng*

Cultural Links

Flowers in the Mirror

Flowers in the Mirror is a fantasy novel written by Li Ruzhen of the Qing Dynasty, who is said to have worked for about 20 years to complete it.

This novel is set in the reign of Empress Wu Zetian. It mainly tells of the overseas traveling experiences of Tang Ao and his companions, as well as the flower fairies' contributions to the court.

Flowers in the Mirror gains much attention for its reflection of the concept of feminism. It fully acknowledges women's talent and social status, appealing for equality between men and women.

Peking opera

Lian Jinfeng is one of the representative Peking operas of the Mei School.

Peking opera is one of the five great opera genres in China, the other four of which are Yue opera, Huangmei opera, Ping opera, and Yu opera. The tunes of Peking opera are mainly *xipi* (loud, sonorous, excited and indignant) and *erhuang* (calm and steady).

Peking opera is the quintessence of Chinese culture. In 2010, it was inscribed on the Representative List of Intangible Cultural Heritage of Humanity by UNESCO.

A stage photo of Mei Lanfang, taken from the Peking opera *The Drunken Beauty*

The Lord of the Rings

The Lord of the Rings is a fantasy novel written by the English writer and linguist J. R. R. Tolkien. It is acknowledged as the forerunner of modern fantasy literature.

The Lord of the Rings mainly tells stories about people of various races in the Middle-Earth, who join together to revolt against the Dark Lord Sauron for freedom.

Discussion

1. What can you learn from Lian Jinfeng?
2. What do you think are the reasons for the popularity of fantasy literature?

廿　廉锦枫

引

1924年，京剧《廉锦枫》在日本上演，主演是梅兰芳。演出大获成功，促成了一部京剧电影的拍摄。这部电影包括梅兰芳两部代表作中的两幕戏，后来在日本各地放映，赢得了日本观众的喜爱。

同上述京剧、电影一样，以下故事也改编自小说《镜花缘》。

◎ 京剧中的廉锦枫由葛香汝饰演

故事

廉锦枫是君子国的孝女。她的父亲在流放中亡故之后，她就独自照顾生病的母亲。得知海参可以治疗母亲的病，她便勤练潜水，定期入海取参。从那以后，母亲的病渐渐康复。

有一天，为了捉海参，她又像平常一样带上宝剑，潜入深海，但这次她却被网住了，一个渔夫和他的妻子正在用这渔网捕鱼。这对夫妇见这个女孩年轻漂亮，就立刻把她捆住，打算将她卖个好价钱。正在那时，一艘大船驶了过来。廉锦枫大声呼救。

一个叫唐敖的秀才正偕友游历各国，恰巧路过。听到有人大声呼救，唐敖和他的朋友们便急速向岸边驶来。

廉锦枫告诉他们："我曾祖本是岭南人。为躲避战乱，他们搬到了君子国。我自幼读了很多诗作。今日，我来此地为母亲取参，不料却被这渔夫捉住。他们要卖了我，请救救我！"为了证明她所说属实，廉锦枫写下一首七言绝句，描述自己的遭遇。

唐敖认为她是个德才兼备的女子，立即取出一百两银子，换取廉锦枫的自由。

为报答唐敖救了她，廉锦枫又跳入海中，与蚌搏斗，取得大珠一颗，赠给了他。

◎ 廉锦枫刺蚌剧照
出自京剧《廉锦枫》

文化链接

《镜花缘》

《镜花缘》是一部奇幻小说，作者是清代的李汝珍。相传他花了大约二十年才完成这部小说。

小说背景设定在女皇武则天统治时期。小说主要讲述了唐敖和同伴在海外游历的经历，以及花仙子们对朝廷的贡献。

《镜花缘》以其所反映的女性主义观念而备受瞩目。它充分承认女性的才能和社会地位，呼吁男女平等。

京剧

《廉锦枫》是梅派京剧代表作之一。

京剧为中国五大戏曲剧种之一，其余四种是越剧、黄梅戏、评剧和豫剧。京剧的腔调主要为西皮（高亢激昂）和二黄（沉着稳重）。

京剧是中国的国粹。2010年，京剧被联合国教科文组织列入《人类非物质文化遗产代表作名录》。

◎ 梅兰芳剧照
出自京剧《贵妃醉酒》

《指环王》

《指环王》是一部奇幻小说，作者是英国作家、语言学家J.R.R.托尔金。它被公认为现代奇幻文学的先驱之作。

《指环王》主要讲述了中土世界各族人民为追求自由而联合起来反抗黑暗魔君索伦的故事。

讨论

1. 从廉锦枫身上，你能学到什么？
2. 你认为奇幻文学受欢迎的原因有哪些？